UNIVERSAL BASIC INCOME

WHAT EVERYONE NEEDS TO KNOW®

UNIVERSAL BASIC INCOME

WHAT EVERYONE NEEDS TO KNOW®

MATT ZWOLINSKI AND
MIRANDA PERRY FLEISCHER

OXFORD
UNIVERSITY PRESS

OXFORD
UNIVERSITY PRESS

Oxford University Press is a department of the University of Oxford. It furthers
the University's objective of excellence in research, scholarship, and education
by publishing worldwide. Oxford is a registered trade mark of Oxford University
Press in the UK and certain other countries.

"What Everyone Needs to Know" is a registered trademark of
Oxford University Press.

Published in the United States of America by Oxford University Press
198 Madison Avenue, New York, NY 10016, United States of America.

Library of Congress Cataloging-in-Publication Data
Names: Zwolinski, Matt, author. | Fleischer, Miranda Perry, author.
Title: Universal basic income : what everyone needs to know /
Matt Zwolinski and Miranda Perry Fleischer.
Description: New York, NY : Oxford University Press, [2023] |
Series: What everyone needs to know | Includes bibliographical
references and index.
Identifiers: LCCN 2023004653 (print) | LCCN 2023004654 (ebook) |
ISBN 9780197556221 (paperback) | ISBN 9780197556252 (hardback) |
ISBN 9780197556245 (epub)
Subjects: LCSH: Basic income.
Classification: LCC HC79.I5 Z96 2023 (print) | LCC HC79.I5 (ebook) |
DDC 362.5/82—dc23/eng/20230208
LC record available at https://lccn.loc.gov/2023004653
LC ebook record available at https://lccn.loc.gov/2023004654

DOI: 10.1093/wentk/9780197556252.001.0001

Paperback printed by Sheridan Books, Inc., United States of America
Hardback printed by Bridgeport National Bindery, Inc., United States of America

Matt
For Jen, always.

Miranda
To my daughter

CONTENTS

Part 6: Objections

Part 7: The Politics of a UBI

ACKNOWLEDGMENTS

Over the years, we have enjoyed and benefited from many conversations with friends and colleagues about the Universal Basic Income (UBI). Supporters of the idea have drawn our attention to advantages we hadn't previously appreciated. And critics have kept us honest, never letting us miss a weak point in an argument or data. We are grateful to the many people who have helped shape the ideas in this book, including Rosanne Altshuler, Anne Alstott, Peter Barnes, Leslie Book, Bryan Caplan, Michael Cholbi, Michelle Drumbl, Ross Emmett, Jessica Flanigan, Evelyn Forget, Natalie Foster, Chris Freiman, David Friedman, David Gamage, David Gillette, Ari Glogower, David Henderson, Chris Hughes, Sarah Lawsky, Ben Leff, Otto Lehto, Susie Morse, Mike Munger, Vida Panitch, Scott Santens, Dan Shaviro, Andrew Stern, Michael Tanner, Justin Tosi, Kevin Vallier, Michael Weber, Derek Yonai, and Larry Zelenak. We are especially indebted to Mario Juarez-Garcia for his thoughtful comments on an earlier draft of this book.

Matt would particularly like to thank Karl Widerquist for drawing his attention to the UBI as a research topic, and Philippe Van Parijs for his decades of path-breaking scholarship, mentorship, and advocacy in this area.

Miranda would like to express extra gratitude to Daniel Hemel, her co-author on two prior UBI articles that sharpened her thoughts and provided the basis for many of the discussions that appear within this book. She is also appreciative of thoughtful and detailed research help from the University of San Diego Law Library, including Liz Parker, Melissa Abernathy, David Isom, Sasha Nuñez, and Julianne Odin; and research assistants Carlisle Olson, Justin Oetting, and Sara Pike.

Finally, we are deeply grateful to Hannah Doyle for her confidence in us to write this book, her patience throughout the challenging years of the Covid-19 pandemic, and her unfailing support and encouragement. Thanks also to Brent Matheny, Joshua McCabe, and an anonymous referee for their careful reading of our manuscript.

INTRODUCTION

Imagine getting $500 from the government, every month, deposited into your bank account. Once received, the money would be yours to do whatever you want with. You could buy groceries, pay for rent or childcare, save it, or blow it all in one big night out. How would a steady stream of income like that change your life? What if everybody in your society got it? How would it change our *world*?

The idea you've just imagined has a name. Or, rather, it has several names. Some people call it a "guaranteed income." Others call it a "basic income." In this book, we'll adopt the most common label used today—a Universal Basic Income, or UBI for short.

As we'll see in this book, the UBI is an idea that's been around for a long time—at least since the 18th century. But there has never been more interest in the idea than there is today. In 2016, Switzerland became the first country ever to hold a nationwide referendum on the UBI. The measure was defeated by a large margin, but this event would turn out to be just the beginning of a global wave of interest in the UBI. The Swiss referendum was followed quickly by pilot programs in Finland, the Netherlands, Scotland, and Ontario.

In the United States, a UBI was the central policy proposal of Andrew Yang's 2020 presidential campaign. Yang's campaign attracted a horde of passionate followers—the "Yang Gang" as they were called—and sparked a nationwide conversation about the merits of a UBI. Today, many of those individuals have gone on to push for a UBI or other forms of cash transfers in different venues. Some are working with the organization Yang founded—Humanity Forward—to advocate a permanent extension of the fully refundable child tax credit—a kind of "UBI for kids." Others are working with Mayors for a Guaranteed Income, an organization that is currently sponsoring more than forty different pilot programs in cities across the United States, from Los Angeles, California, to Providence, Rhode Island.

So, if the idea of a UBI has been around for several centuries, why is there suddenly so much interest in it today? The current popularity of the UBI does not seem to be due to any single factor or issue. But there does seem to be a *cluster* of issues related to economic insecurity which, taken together, have convinced a lot of people that the time is right for a UBI.

Increasing inequality and stubbornly resistant pockets of poverty are one set of issues that have captured many people's attention. Developed economies are growing wealthier, but that wealth seems to be becoming more and more concentrated in a smaller number of hands, while the economic well-being of workers and the unemployed stagnates or in some cases declines. Merely tinkering with existing welfare programs seems unlikely to make a significant difference. A UBI would constitute a radical shift in our approach to shrinking inequality and dramatically reducing poverty.

We also live in a world where the future of work is radically uncertain. Advances in technology and artificial intelligence (AI) have led to machines doing work that only humans used to be able to do. And the trend is likely to continue at an accelerated pace. At a minimum, these technological developments will be highly disruptive, putting many people out of work and leaving them struggling to find alternative employment. At worst, there simply might not *be* any sources of alternative employment once AI gets smart enough. What does a welfare state look like in a world without work? A UBI represents one possible way forward.

Finally, some people are simply fed up with the expense, paternalism, and complexity of existing welfare systems. Do we really need hundreds of different social welfare programs at the federal, state, and local level? Do we really need a welfare system built on the assumption that poor people can't be trusted to make their own decisions about what to buy? A UBI strikes many as a simpler, more efficient, and more respectful way of helping the poor than our current system.

Of course, the UBI is not without its critics. In fact, one of the interesting features of the debate over the UBI is the polarization of opinion on the topic. There are a lot of books out there that are *passionately* in support of a UBI. And there are a lot of critics who argue that a UBI would be a moral and economic catastrophe. They argue that a UBI would be ridiculously expensive. People would stop working. People would blow the money on drugs, alcohol, and gambling. A UBI is the first step on a slippery slope toward communism. And so on.

What's too often missing from this debate is serious analysis that recognizes both the advantages *and* the drawbacks of a UBI. And that is precisely what we hope to provide you with in this book. Both of us are on the record as supporting a UBI, all-things-considered. But neither of us is suffering from any illusions regarding the potential problems with the policy. Our goal in this book is not to convince you to become a supporter of the UBI, or to oppose it. Rather, we want to provide you with the most accurate information possible about the arguments, evidence, insights, and weaknesses from both sides of the debate, so that you can make up your own mind about the issue in an intelligent way.

As a political philosopher and an expert in the law and economics of taxation and welfare policy, we're in a unique position to guide you through both the "big ideas" of the UBI and the nuts-and-bolts of policy design. It's important to think about whether a UBI would be fair or equitable, or compatible with respect for the dignity and worth of the individual. But it's also important to know how it would *work*. How much would it realistically cost? How would it be funded? How would it be administered? Would it vary based on wealth, regional cost-of-living differences, or family composition? Too often, detailed issues of policy design are neglected in discussions about the UBI. Our book takes these issues seriously, and presents a range of possible approaches for designing a UBI that works.

Our book is organized into seven parts. Part 1 provides a brief overview of the UBI—what it is, where the idea came from, where it's been tried, and what the main arguments for and against it are. Part 2 dives right into questions of policy detail. How big would a UBI be, who would be eligible, how would it be delivered, and more. Part 3 compares the UBI with alternative social welfare policies such as the Earned Income Tax Credit (EITC), the Negative Income Tax (NIT), and traditional welfare programs like food stamps, which are now administered through the Supplemental Nutrition Assistance Program (SNAP). Part 4 discusses the results of various experiments with the UBI. Part 5 discusses potential advantages of a UBI, and part 6 discusses some common objections. Finally, part 7 explores the politics of a UBI—which groups support it, which oppose it, and what chance does it have of actually becoming policy?

Throughout the book, we compare a UBI with a range of alternative social welfare programs. Most of those policies will be drawn from the United States, since that is the country with which both of us are most familiar. But many of the lessons that we draw from these comparisons—in-kind vs. cash transfers, means-tested vs. non-means-tested programs—generalize to other countries as well. We think these comparisons will help you gain a better understanding of the distinctive features of a UBI, even if you are unfamiliar with or not particularly interested in the US welfare system.

We wrote this book to serve as a resource for people who want to gain a better understanding of the UBI. And we've tried to make it as useful and as flexible a resource as possible. If you want, you can read the whole thing from cover to cover. But each chapter in this book is a self-contained answer to a specific question about the UBI. So if you just want to know, say, how a UBI would affect people's willingness to work, feel free to skip right to chapter 49, and read that answer on its own. Sometimes, in answering a question, we'll refer to ideas or data that we discuss elsewhere in the book. When we do that, we've provided cross-references to make it easy for you to jump straight to the relevant parts of the book. Finally, if you ever encounter a technical term or abbreviation (what's SNAP again?) with which you're not familiar, you can turn to the glossary at the end of the book for a brief definition.

So, after all that, let's start with a seemingly simple question. Just what *is* a UBI, anyway?

Part 1

THE BASICS

1

WHAT IS A BASIC INCOME?

A lot of confusion about the concept of a UBI results from people talking about it as though it was a single, precisely defined policy proposal. We think it's more helpful to think of the UBI as a *family* of proposals. All versions of a UBI have three key elements in common. Beyond those common elements, however, the differences between various proposals can be enormous, so much so that asking whether someone supports "a UBI" is almost a meaningless question. The real question is: what *kind* of UBI—if any—do you support?

The first thing all UBI proposals have in common is that they involve unrestricted *cash transfers*. Most other government programs provide what are called "in-kind" benefits—free or discounted access to various types of goods and services. Medicaid provides the poor with access to medical care and prescription drugs. SNAP provides access to food. Government programs that do provide cash often restrict where it can be spent. A UBI, in contrast, gives people cash that they can use in any way they see fit.

Second, the cash transfers that a UBI provides are *unconditional* in nature. What this means is that recipients' eligibility to receive the money is not dependent on whether they're working or not, whether they're trying to find work, or why they can't work. This, as we'll see, is one of the most sharply distinguishing features of a UBI compared with alternative social welfare policies. It is also one of the most controversial.

Finally, a UBI is often said to be "universal," in the sense that everybody gets it, rich and poor alike. In fact, this is often taken to be the *central* defining feature of a UBI. Universality is, after all, the

"U" in "UBI." On closer inspection, however, universality turns out to be a somewhat tricky concept to pin down. No UBI proposal that we have seen actually recommends giving the money to *everyone*. National UBI proposals, for instance, limit eligibility to citizens, or at least to permanent residents. Many proposals limit the UBI to adults, excluding children. And while most proponents of a UBI *say* that eligibility for the grant is not dependent on income or wealth, we'll let you in on a little secret: nobody really means this.

Here's why. A UBI that gave money to everybody would either be so expensive as to be unmanageable, or so small as to be practically useless to the people who need it most. In order to provide a reasonably sized grant to the people who need it most, you simply have to use some sort of means testing (to use a "means test" is to limit benefits to individuals or households under a certain income threshold). Some proposals do this on the front-end, only issuing checks to people whose income falls below a certain threshold. That's how a Negative Income Tax (NIT) works—see chapter 29. But if you don't means test on the front end, you need to do it on the back end. In other words, you give *everybody* a check, but then you tax some or all of the benefit back from people whose income exceeds a certain level. Such a program is still universal in a *sense*. But also, sort of, not really.

Beyond these three very broad features, there is a *lot* of variation among UBI proposals. And as they say, "the Devil is in the details." Whether a UBI would be a good idea or not probably depends a lot more on how these details are fleshed out than on the broad characteristics that all UBIs share.

For instance, one important question is how *large* the UBI will be. Above, we used an example of a UBI of $500 per month. As we'll see, this is a pretty common proposal. But some people have proposed much larger UBIs, and some people have proposed smaller ones.

How large a UBI ought to be will depend, in part, on what you think a UBI is *for*. Is the purpose of a UBI to supplement the income of people working in low-wage jobs? Is it to provide a steady stream of income for the temporarily unemployed? Or is the goal of a UBI to provide a *permanent* income, a way for people to meet their basic needs without ever having to work another day in their life? A relatively modest UBI might be sufficient to meet the first two goals. But the third would require a significantly more generous grant.

A closely related issue involves how we would go about *paying for a UBI*. Giving $500 per month to every one of the 330 million or so people currently living in the United States would cost almost $2 trillion per year—a significant amount of money! Should we pay for it by taxing personal income? Taxing corporations? Cutting other programs? Obviously, the larger the UBI, the more pressing and difficult this question becomes.

There's also the question of who is *eligible to receive* the UBI. Most proposals view the UBI as an *individual* entitlement. That is, they envision the UBI being paid to each individual person, and not to families or households. But should a UBI be given to children or only to adults? Should it be given to anybody living in the country, or only citizens or permanent residents? Should felons receive it? Should there be an income cutoff?

We'll explore all these questions in the rest of this book. For now, though, we can understand the UBI as a family of loosely related policies all of which involve direct, unconditional, and sort-of universal cash transfers.

So, you might be asking, where did this idea come from?

2

WHO FIRST THOUGHT
OF THE IDEA?

We're glad you asked!

The idea of a UBI has been around for a surprisingly long time. In fact, one of the first people to propose a basic income was one of the Founding Fathers of the United States. In 1796, Thomas Paine published a pamphlet titled *Agrarian Justice* in which he proposed to

> create a national fund, out of which there shall be paid to every person, when arrived at the age of twenty-one years, the sum of fifteen pounds sterling . . . And also, the sum of ten pounds per annum, during life, to every person now living, of the age of fifty years, and to all others as they shall arrive at that age.[1]

Paine thought of these payments not as a form of charity or welfare but as a kind of "compensation" to which individuals were entitled as a matter of right. What exactly was he trying to compensate people for? Well, Paine believed that the land "in its natural, uncultivated state" was "the common property of the human race." In other words, each of us has a natural human right to the free use of the earth. Over time, however, much of the earth's land has been converted into private property. That has been great in terms of incentivizing people to put the land to productive use. And Paine thought that individuals are completely entitled to keep whatever they produce with their own labor. But the land itself isn't the product of anybody's labor. And so if humanity is going to let private individuals keep that land for their own personal use, those individuals owe humanity fair compensation for that privilege. See chapter 63 for further discussion of this argument.

A similar argument would later be made by Henry George, whose 1879 bestseller *Progress and Poverty* would argue that this compensation could fund a "Single Tax" sufficient to fund all the legitimate activities of government.[2] And, more recently, Peter Barnes has expanded Paine's idea by arguing humanity should be paid dividends based not merely on the value of land, but also the atmosphere, and even the infrastructure of our financial system.[3]

Almost immediately after it was published, however, Paine's proposal was subjected to vigorous criticism. In a 1797 pamphlet titled *The Rights of Infants*, an English schoolteacher named Thomas Spence argued that while Paine's proposal was based on a "great fundamental truth," it would nevertheless leave "multitudes of the people . . . poor and beggarly."[4] Spence identified two specific problems with Paine's idea. First, the only people who qualified for a regular income under it were the elderly. Children received nothing, and adults received only a one-time payment that might quickly be used up. Second, Spence thought, the level of the income was too small to eradicate poverty.

To correct these problems, Spence proposed that the value of all land and houses be divided evenly among the community. The value to be distributed would include not only the unimproved value of natural resources, but the value of all improvements as well. And the beneficiaries of this distribution would include not merely the elderly but everyone, "whether male or female; married or single; legitimate or illegitimate; from a day old to the extremest age; making no difference between the families of rich farmers and merchants." Spence's proposal was thus more *universal* than Paine's and established more of a regular *income* for its beneficiaries. In both of these ways, Spence's model more closely resembles the modern idea of a UBI.

The idea of a UBI would resurface again and again over the course of the 20th century. In England, the philosopher Bertrand Russell endorsed the idea in his 1918 book, *Roads to Freedom*, and the economist James Meade advocated what he called a "social dividend" in his 1989 *Agathotopia: The Economics of Partnership*.[5] In the United States, a UBI found support from an ideologically diverse range of economists, including John Kenneth Galbraith, James Tobin, Milton

Friedman, and Friedrich Hayek, many of whom championed a variation of a UBI called a "Negative Income Tax."[6] Influenced by these scholars, President Richard Nixon championed something akin to a UBI in 1969, although ultimately his proposal was defeated in Congress. We'll have more to say about Nixon's "Family Assistance Plan" in chapter 64.

In his last book, *Where Do We Go From Here?*, published in 1967, Martin Luther King Jr. wrote that "I am now convinced that the simplest approach will prove to be the most effective—the solution to poverty is to abolish it directly by a now widely discussed measure: the guaranteed income . . . The dignity of the individual will flourish when the decisions concerning his life are in his own hands, when he has the assurance that his income is stable and certain, and when he knows that he has the means to seek self-improvement."[7]

From civil rights leader Martin Luther King Jr. to libertarian economist Milton Friedman to founding father Thomas Paine, we can see that the idea of a UBI has always attracted an ideologically diverse group of supporters.

But what about today?

3

WHO ARE SOME RECENT SUPPORTERS OF A BASIC INCOME?

So, the idea of a UBI has been around for a long, long time. But over the course of the last decade or so, interest in the UBI has simply *exploded*.

The first signs of that explosion occurred in Switzerland in 2016. In that year, the country held a national referendum on the UBI, and for a while it looked like there was a decent chance that Switzerland would be the first country to adopt a permanent, national UBI. Ultimately, voters rejected the measure by an overwhelming ratio of 3 to 1. But that may have had less to do with opposition to a UBI as such than with perceived flaws in the particular proposal under consideration. Some of the referendum's supporters suggested that the UBI should be set at a level equivalent to roughly US $2,500 per month per adult. With an estimated price tag of over 200 billion francs annually, this would cost more than three times the entire Federal budget of Switzerland—an amount equal to almost one third of the Swiss GDP!

In the United States, the person most responsible for stimulating recent popular interest in the UBI is Andrew Yang. In 2020, Yang made a surprisingly successful run in the Democratic presidential primaries, based largely on his signature policy of a UBI of $1,000 per month for every American over the age of 18. Although ultimately unsuccessful, Yang's campaign attracted a wide and passionate group of followers (the "Yang Gang") and transformed what had previously been a somewhat obscure idea into part of the mainstream political conversation.

Yang's followers illustrate one of the most fascinating aspects of the UBI movement: the passionate, wholehearted intensity that grips many of the idea's supporters. Long-time UBI advocate Scott Santens, for example, is so committed to UBI that he champions it as a full-time job; he is now one of its most vocal advocates on Twitter and elsewhere. And how does he support himself financially? He crowdsourced himself his own UBI, of course.

Although Yang's candidacy catapulted UBI into the national spotlight, the idea had already been gaining steam across the political spectrum throughout the 21st century. Before Yang championed a UBI as the solution to widespread technological unemployment, labor leader Andy Stern made the same point in his 2016 book, *Raising the Floor*.[1] A former president of the Service Employees International Union, Stern feared that continuing advances in artificial intelligence would lead to a future in which many ordinary people are unable to get good, dependable jobs. A UBI, he speculated, might not just be an option but a *necessity* in a future without work. Meanwhile, on the right, American Enterprise Institute scholar Charles Murray advocated a UBI as a more efficient and humane replacement for what he saw as an expensive, convoluted, and paternalistic welfare state in his 2006 book, *In Our Hands*.[2]

Behind the scenes, a handful of scholars have been writing for decades about the advantages of a UBI. The Belgian philosopher Philippe Van Parijs has been called the "godfather" of the UBI movement and has been writing about the UBI since at least the late 1980s. His 2017 book, *Basic Income: A Radical Proposal for a Free Society and a Sane Economy* is perhaps the most thorough and detailed scholarly defense of the proposal available.[3] Another philosopher, Karl Widerquist, has written voluminously on almost every aspect of the UBI debate, as well as serving as one of the founding editors of the academic journal *Basic Income Studies*.[4] Guy Standing, Anne Lowrey, Evelyn Forget, and Rutger Bregman have also written numerous books and articles on the UBI.[5]

Today, those academic ideas are catching on not just nationally but globally. But has anyone actually implemented a UBI yet?

4

SO, HAS A BASIC INCOME EVER BEEN TRIED?

Well, sort of. At the time of this writing, one US state, one country, and several Native American tribes have something close to a UBI. Although these three cases are each unusual in their own way, they—along with a number of other cash transfer programs and small-scale experiments—can help us better understand how a large-scale, permanent UBI might work.

First, the US state. Since 1982, Alaska has issued annual cash payments to every resident under a program called the Alaska Permanent Fund Dividend. This program has been incredibly popular with residents, and does not appear to have produced any of the negative effects generally associated with a UBI by critics. We'll tell you more about that program in chapter 32.

Next, the country. And this one might surprise you. The only country in the world to have adopted a UBI is . . . the Islamic Republic of Iran! Here's the backstory. In 2010, Iranian president Mahmoud Ahmadinejad made heavy cuts to government subsidies for bread and gas. To compensate, the government adopted a program of direct cash transfers, amounting to approximately 29% of median household income, or about $1.50 extra per person, per day. Originally, these subsidies were to be made only to poorer Iranian citizens, but technical difficulties in estimating income and dissatisfaction from those who would be excluded eventually led the government to opt for a universal benefit instead. The first payments under the program were issued in 2011, and they continue to this day, albeit at lower amounts. The program has received intense criticism from businesses and others who believe it disincentivizes work. But a 2018 study by economists found this criticism unjustified, concluding that "the program did not affect labor supply in any appreciable way."[1]

Finally, many Native American tribes distribute casino revenues on a UBI-like per capita basis. For example, the Eastern Band of Cherokee Indians has done this since 1996. In that year, the tribe opened a casino and decided to distribute a portion of the revenues to all adult tribal members on an equalized, per-capita basis. Payments are made every six months, with an average annual value of approximately $4,000—making it by far the most generous of the three programs we've discussed here. And the results of these payments seem generally positive. One study found payments to be associated with an extra year of educational attainment by age 21, as well as a reduction in crime rates.[2]

We can also learn about how a UBI might work from looking at programs that involve other cash transfers, even if those transfers aren't fully unconditional or universal. For example, the *Oportunidades* program in Mexico and the *Bolsa Familia* program in Brazil have provided cash assistance to families for decades. In both cases, however, the assistance is conditional and less than fully universal. The programs target families with children, and parents will only receive the money if their children regularly attend school and receive certain forms of preventative health care.

In addition to these long-standing programs, governments around the world have occasionally run shorter-term experiments with various kinds of cash transfers. The most famous set of experiments ran for over a decade in the United States between 1968 and 1982. These experiments were designed to test the idea of a Negative Income Tax at a time when the Nixon administration was seriously considering implementing the idea. Ultimately, the plan was abandoned. We'll explain how a Negative Income Tax compares to a UBI in chapter 29, and we'll have much more to say about these experiments in chapter 33.

Around the same time, the Canadian government was experimenting with its own Minimum Income (or MINCOME) project. Between 1974 and 1978 in Dauphin, Manitoba, low-income families received an unconditional cash grant from the Canadian government. The results of this experiment were buried for decades after the program was shut down following a change in government.

But an economist named Evelyn Forget dug them up, and as we'll see in chapter 34, discovered some deeply interesting and important findings.

Starting in the 1980s, interest in the UBI began to stall. But over the last decade or so a wave of more recent experiments has taken place. The idea has struck a special chord in California's Silicon Valley, and leaders in the tech industry have been some of the idea's most vocal and most financially supportive proponents in recent years. Sam Altman of the startup accelerator Y Combinator saw potential in the idea, and recently launched a $60 million project to test it by providing cash grants to several thousand families. And Facebook co-founder Chris Hughes joined with Natalie Foster to start the Economic Security Project, an organization devoted to UBI advocacy and experimentation. That organization is now working with another—Mayors for a Guaranteed Income—which has sponsored pilot programs in cities across the United States, from Stockton, California, to Baltimore, Maryland.

And it's not just the United States. The Finnish government ran a two-year pilot of a guaranteed income program, and similar experiments have been run in the Netherlands, Scotland, and Germany. Intriguingly, one of the longest-term experiments in the world is actually being run by a private entity. The charitable organization GiveDirectly is running a twelve-year, $30 million basic income program in rural Kenya! We'll have lots to say about this and other pilot programs in part 4 of this book.

5

WHAT ARE THE MAIN ARGUMENTS IN FAVOR OF A BASIC INCOME?

As we have seen, the idea of a UBI has been around for a long time. And over that time, a great variety of arguments have developed in its support. Most of the arguments, however, fall into one of six main categories. The first three focus on the consequences of a UBI; the final three on more fundamental values.

1) **Automation**—The most recent and most currently influential argument focuses on artificial intelligence and the increasing automation of work. This idea was at the core of Andrew Yang's 2020 presidential campaign, and it also underlies support for the UBI among many of Silicon Valley's tech elite and some labor leaders such as Andy Stern.[1] The argument comes in two forms: one relatively moderate, the other quite radical. In its moderate form, the argument claims that technological unemployment will pose severe transitional problems. People who are put out of work because their job has been taken over by a computer will need help with retraining, relocating, and getting back on their feet. A UBI can provide a cushion to make that transition easier.

The more radical argument claims that the problem posed by technological unemployment will be not transitional but permanent. We may be entering an era where there simply *won't be any jobs left*, at least for large numbers of people without highly specialized training. On this view, the purpose of a UBI is not merely to serve as a temporary cushion, but rather as a permanent means of support—to replace income from work, rather than to supplement it. We'll have more to say about this argument in chapter 38.

2) **Efficiency**—Most people want government programs to be efficient, rather than wasteful. In other words, they want those programs to produce as much benefit as possible for every dollar they spend. And this looks like it might be a good reason to support a UBI, as we discuss more in chapter 41. For starters, cash transfers are generally more efficient than in-kind programs. Giving someone $100 worth of food stamps is great if food happens to be the thing they really need most. But if what they really need is to pay their rent, or to buy bus fare, then they would have been better off with cash. Cash transfers allow individuals to make their own decisions about what they need most. And if we assume that most people know their own needs better than the government does, then there is good reason to think we'll make a bigger improvement in people's lives by giving them cash rather than goods and services. A UBI might also enhance efficiency by streamlining and simplifying the way government provides aid to the needy—a point emphasized by Charles Murray in his defense of a UBI.[2] Right now there are over one hundred different programs at the Federal level designed to fight poverty in various ways, many of which could be consolidated into a single cash transfer program. Not only would that cut down on government bureaucracy, but it would also make it considerably easier for the people targeted by those programs to obtain the benefits to which they are entitled—by cutting down on paperwork, travel between different offices, dealing with different caseworkers, and so on.

3) **Poverty and Inequality**—If you're reading this book, chances are you live in a very wealthy society. Not just wealthy compared to other countries today, but wealthier than almost any other nation in the entire *history* of the world. Why, then, is there still so much poverty in our midst? If we're so rich, why should we allow anyone to be poor? A UBI would almost certainly help to reduce poverty significantly. *Eliminating* poverty is a trickier question, one which we will take up later in this book (see chapter 39). We'll also talk in chapter 40 about how a UBI will affect inequality,

which is a different issue from poverty. A UBI establishes a *minimum* income, but it doesn't by itself set any kind of maximum on how much somebody can earn. Still, if a UBI is paid for by taxes on people with relatively higher incomes, and if most of the benefits go to people whose incomes are lower, the net effect should be to reduce inequality overall.

4) **Respect**—The efficiency argument for cash transfers depends on the assumption that if we give people choice, they will generally make better decisions about their own lives than the government would. But not everybody accepts this assumption. In fact, many people seem to think that poverty is evidence of some kind of character defect such as bad judgment, weakness of will, or simple laziness. What the poor need, on this view, is someone to make their decisions for them: to limit their choices and to guide them toward virtue. As we discuss in chapter 42, advocates of a UBI reject this sort of paternalism and instead urge respect for all individuals as autonomous moral agents. They argue that poverty is often a result of structural factors rather than individual moral failing. And they argue that even when individual character is an issue, the best way to develop it is to give people the freedom to take responsibility for their own lives. Paternalism is not only inefficient; it is fundamentally disrespectful.

5) **Freedom**—One of the most fundamental arguments for a UBI is based on the value of freedom. Advocates of a UBI believe that everyone should be able to live their lives as they see fit, without undue interference from others. But freedom is a luxury the poor often cannot afford. Someone who is living paycheck to paycheck often has no real choice but to comply with the dictates of their boss. Someone who is financially dependent on their spouse often has no real choice but to stay in that relationship no matter how dysfunctional it may become.[3] A UBI gives people freedom not merely in the formal sense of a legally protected right, but what the philosopher Philippe Van Parijs has called "real freedom," or the genuine *capacity* to live their lives as they choose.[4] By providing assistance to those in need, a UBI lifts people out of the desperation and vulnerability to exploitation of poverty. And by providing that assistance in the form of cash, a UBI gives people

maximum discretion to live their lives according to their own choices. We'll see this value reappear throughout the book.

6) **Compensation**—Finally, some people have argued that a UBI might be justified as a way of compensating people for ways in which society has harmed them. This argument has a variety of forms, but we'll mention two common ones here. The first springs from the idea that natural resources like land and minerals are, from a moral perspective, the common property of humanity. On this view, those who have been lucky enough to convert those resources into wealth shouldn't be the sole beneficiaries of that wealth. Sure, they can keep a bit extra to compensate themselves for their labor, but they owe the rest of us compensation for the use of these resources. We'll have more to say about this argument in chapter 59.

The second argument, one that reappears in chapter 43, is that a UBI might help to compensate certain groups within society for the lingering effects of past injustices. The guiding idea here is that policies like slavery, colonialism, and legally enforced segregation can produce harms that last long after the laws themselves have been abolished. Many of the most disadvantaged groups in today's societies are still suffering the after-effects of these injustices. And since we as a society were the ones who caused those harms, we have a responsibility to do what we can to make things right. A UBI can never make the victims of social injustice whole again. But by redistributing resources toward the most economically disadvantaged individuals within a society, it can at least make some progress toward this end.

6

WHAT ARE THE MAIN ARGUMENTS AGAINST A BASIC INCOME?

Not everyone thinks that a UBI would be a good idea. In particular, there are three objections that occur to almost everyone who considers a UBI. This section presents those objections, plus a fourth which, while less common, nevertheless raises an important issue.

1. **Cost**—How much is it going to cost? This is the first question almost everyone has about a UBI. And with good reason. Depending on how it is structured, a UBI could be very, very expensive. Let's do some quick math. There are about 260 million adults living in the United States. Suppose we wanted to provide all adults with a UBI of $1,000 per month. That's a decent amount of money, but not quite enough to clear the poverty threshold for a single individual (that would require just under $14,000 annually, according to 2022 US Census Bureau guidelines). The cost of such a program would be approximately $3.1 trillion—more than the Federal government spent in 2021 on Social Security, Medicare, and Medicaid combined, and almost half of the entire Federal budget for that same year! There are ways of reducing the cost of a UBI, as we'll see in parts 2 and 6 of this book. Still, proponents of a UBI face a challenging dilemma. The amount paid by a UBI needs to be large enough to make a real difference in people's lives, but small enough that its total cost is not overwhelming. Achieving both of these goals simultaneously is no easy task.

2. **Work**—The second objection that most people have to a UBI is that it will lead people to stop working. Unlike other social welfare policies like the EITC, a UBI gives people money whether they're working or not. Won't this cause people to work less, or even to stop working altogether? Early experiments with a Negative Income Tax initially seemed to confirm this concern, and some have argued that recent extensions of unemployment insurance during the Covid-19 pandemic produced the same consequence, for the same reason. We will have more to say about this worry in part 6. Before moving on to the third objection, however, there is a related concern about the UBI and work that is worth mentioning. Most people have no problem with the state providing assistance to those who are genuinely unable to support themselves. But people's attitude toward those who are able but *unwilling* to work is a different matter. Such people are often looked down upon as "free-loaders," and many if not most people think that the state has no obligation to support them. But the UBI gives money to everybody—it does not attempt to discriminate between the "deserving" and the "undeserving" poor. And many people see this as a serious flaw. We'll examine this specific objection in more depth in chapter 50.

3. **Wasting Cash**—A third common objection to a UBI is that people will just waste cash. If you give people money that they can use whichever way they want, won't they squander it on drugs, alcohol, and gambling? This type of distrust is one large reason many welfare programs have traditionally provided in-kind or restricted benefits, such as food stamps or housing vouchers.

It is true that some people will fritter a UBI away, just as some people find a way to trade in-kind benefits like food stamps for drugs or alcohol. But evidence from existing cash transfer problems and UBI experiments suggests that this should not be a huge concern, as we'll see throughout the book. And we'll look at this specific objection more closely in chapter 51.

4. **Making the Poor Worse Off**—A final objection raises a less obvious, but deeply important concern: could a UBI actually make the poor *worse* off? As we have seen above, a UBI has the potential to be incredibly expensive. Those on the far left of the political spectrum

might be comfortable with this added expense, but conservatives and moderates almost certainly will not be. As a political matter, then, the only way to attract sufficient support for a UBI is probably going to involve funding it (at least in part) by cutting other programs. And there's the rub. As Robert Greenstein of the Center for Budget and Policy Priorities puts it, "If you take dollars targeted on people in the bottom fifth or two-fifths of the population and convert them to universal payments to people all the way up the income scale, you're redistributing *upward*. That would increase poverty and inequality rather than reduce them."[1] We'll talk more about this objection in chapter 53, and about whether a UBI actually redistributes upward in chapter 8.

Part 2

HOW WOULD IT WORK?

7

HOW BIG WOULD IT BE?

So, exactly how big would a UBI be?[1] Well, that depends. The most well-known proposals in the United States cluster around two figures.[2] At the high end, labor leader Andy Stern, basic income activist Scott Santens, libertarian Charles Murray, and 2020 presidential candidate Andrew Yang have proposed transfers of $1,000 per month, as did the Chicago mayoral task force. Scholar Philippe Van Parijs and co-author Yannick Vanderborght suggest that a country's UBI should be 25% of its per-capita gross domestic product, which would be about $1,200 per month in the United States.[3]

At the lower end, Facebook co-founder Chris Hughes and one of the authors of this book have proposed transfers of $500 per month; the Stockton experiment uses this sum as well. Although these two figures may seem miles apart, they aren't really—most of the $1,000-per-month proposals exclude children. A $1,000-per-month UBI paid only to adults is comparable to a $500-per-month UBI paid to a two-parent family of four; a single mother of two is worse off with a $1,000 UBI paid only to adults than with a $500 UBI paid to adults and children alike.

Is this enough to end poverty as we know it, as many advocates hope a UBI will do? For context, the 2022 poverty line in the contiguous United States was $13,590;[4] the cut-off for "deep poverty" was half that. At first glance, it looks like a monthly UBI of $1,000 or $500 per month could make a substantial dent in poverty and/or deep poverty, respectively.

But determining whether individuals are lifted "out of poverty" by a UBI is trickier than it seems, as we'll see in chapter 39. First, there is nothing magical about these definitions. The poverty level is defined as three times the cost of a "minimum food diet," and the deep poverty level is simply half that. These numbers don't reflect geographical variations in the cost of living, or individual differences in needs for health and child care expenses.

Moreover, only some sources of income "count" when determining whether one is below the poverty line. For example, unemployment compensation counts toward one's income, but SNAP benefits and refundable tax credits like the EITC do not. Imagine that someone receiving $500 per month of benefits that do not count as income begins receiving a $500-per-month UBI that does count as income. Her "official" income would rise by $500 per month, even though her material well-being might stay the same or only improve marginally.

But even if a UBI did not "end poverty," several US studies suggest that even smaller unconditional cash transfers yield significant benefits. As discussed in chapter 4, the Eastern Cherokee casino payments (roughly $4,000 per year) are associated with increased years of schooling and lower crime rates; the Alaska Permanent Fund Dividend (approximately $2,000 per year) is associated with a reduction in low-birth-weight babies (see chapter 32).[5]

A $500-per-month UBI—and certainly a $1,000-per-month UBI—could therefore substantially improve the lives of millions. But neither can completely alleviate the concerns of those worried about automation rendering most jobs obsolete. As of May 2022, average *weekly* earnings for US manufacturing workers were just over $1,000.[6] Even a basic income of $1,000 *per month* only partially lessens the sting of being replaced by a robot; a UBI of $500 per month, even less so.

On the other hand, a $500-per-month UBI is less likely to negatively impact work incentives (as we discuss in chapter 49). Although some working-age adults may be willing to live on an income roughly equivalent to a $3-per-hour full-time wage in order to not work, it's hard to imagine that substantial numbers will make that trade-off. This does not undercut the point that even a small UBI can greatly improve well-being. For many individuals, $500 per month is simply the difference between repairing a broken-down car versus losing one's job due to lack of transportation, and not a pathway to a life spent surfing at the beach.

Back to the original question: The size of a UBI will depend on several trade-offs and value judgments. If we implement a UBI, should we maintain or minimize existing welfare programs? How much inefficiency from any increased taxes are we willing to bear? If we incur deficits to finance a UBI, how should we evaluate the trade-offs between the interests of present and future generations? And finally, how do we as a society determine how much redistribution is ethically justified?

8

WOULD RICH PEOPLE RECEIVE A BASIC INCOME?

If a UBI is "universal," does that mean millionaires and billionaires—in addition to minimum-wage workers—would receive one? Superficially, the answer depends on whom you ask and how you structure it. But upon closer inspection, we see that under most scenarios, wealthier folks wouldn't financially benefit from a UBI, even if they appear to "receive" a transfer from the government.

Some advocates, including Philippe Van Parijs and Yannick Vanderborght, argue that a truly "universal" basic income must not be "subjected to an income or means test."[1] (A "means test" means that a benefit varies with income.) To them, a key benefit of a UBI is that it is *not* targeted to the poor. Its universal nature reduces stigma, enhances the dignity of the poor, and creates a sense of community among all citizens. On this view, every citizen, rich and poor alike, would receive an identical sum. If *Ava*, *Ben*, and *Christine* live in a country that implements a $500-per-month UBI, then their individual net worths each increase by $6,000 per year, regardless of their financial circumstances.

Other advocates, such as Charles Murray and Chris Hughes, propose UBIs that vary with income. This can be done two ways. One method—advocated by Charles Murray—is via a recapture tax. The other is to use an explicit *ex ante* phase-out, as most existing welfare programs do. These are mathematically similar.

To illustrate, first imagine a UBI of $6,000 that phases out at a rate of 10% starting with one's first dollar of non-UBI income, and fully phases out once income hits $60,000 (10% × $60,000 = $6,000):

- *Ava*, who earns $0, receives a UBI of $6,000 for a net transfer from the government of $6,000;
- *Ben*, who earns $30,000, receives a UBI of $3,000 (his UBI phases out by $3,000, which is 10% of $30,000) for a net transfer from the government to *Ben* of $3,000; and
- *Christine*, who earns $100,000, receives no UBI (her UBI phases out completely; 10% of $60,000 = $6,000) for a net transfer of zero.

This is identical to a UBI that is paid to all but "recaptured" *ex post* with a 10% tax (in addition to the regular income tax) imposed on all non-UBI income until the UBI has been repaid (which occurs once income hits $60,000 (10% × $60,000 = $6,000)). Here,

- *Ava*, who earns $0, receives a UBI of $6,000 and pays no recapture tax, for a net transfer from the government of $6,000;
- *Ben*, who earns $30,000, receives a UBI of $6,000 but pays a recapture tax of $3,000 (10% of $30,000) for a net transfer from the government to *Ben* of $3,000; and
- *Christine*, who earns $100,000, receives a UBI of $6,000 but pays a recapture tax of $6,000 (10% of $60,000 = $6,000) for a net transfer of zero.

Stopping here, it *appears* that a very real difference exists between advocates who would phase-out or recapture a UBI from higher-income individuals, and those who reject means tests. It seems that the latter would increase even Jeff Bezos's bank account by $6,000 every year; the former would not. But these examples do not tell the full story.

First, as one of us has argued elsewhere, any decently sized UBI proposal would realistically require some across-the-board increases in income or consumption taxes (that is, increases that would apply to all, as opposed to recapture taxes that are capped at the size of the UBI).[2] And a UBI that is financed by an across-the-board income tax has the same effect as a cash transfer subject to an income test: because one's tax bill will increase as income rises, the net amount of UBI received will decrease.[3] Whether a UBI explicitly phases out or is paid to all is therefore a distinction without a difference in most instances.

To illustrate, imagine a UBI of $6,000 paid to all regardless of income coupled with a surtax of 10% tax on *all* other income, with no exemption amount. Unlike the example above, this surtax does not disappear once the UBI is repaid:

- *Ava*, who earns $0, receives a UBI payment of $6,000 and pays no tax, resulting in a net transfer from the government to *Ava* of $6,000;
- *Ben*, who earns $30,000, receives a UBI payment of $6,000 but pays tax of $3,000 (10% of $30,000), resulting in a net transfer of $3,000; and
- *Christine*, who earns $100,000, receives a UBI payment of $6,000 but pays tax of $10,000 (10% of $100,000), resulting in a net transfer from *Christine* to the government of $4,000.

We can see that for *Ava* and *Ben*, this format is mathematically identical to the prior two. And both here and in the prior examples, an additional dollar of income would reduce the net payment they receive. What differs is *Christine*'s treatment. Here, she appears to benefit because she receives a full $6,000 benefit from the UBI. But this benefit is more than overshadowed by the additional $10,000 she now pays in taxes, with the result that she is now $4,000 worse off than she was in the previous two examples.

This illustrates a potential problem with trying to explicitly limit a UBI to lower-income individuals via a phase-out or tax that disappears once the UBI has been recaptured. When benefits fall as income rises, this has the same negative effect on work incentives as a tax. If earning an additional $1,000 in wages costs you $500, it doesn't matter whether the $500 takes the form of taxes or lost benefits. Either way, the actual benefits of working are reduced—but only for those lower-income individuals below the phase-out or recapture threshold, like *Ava* and *Ben*. Individuals above the threshold are unaffected by a phase-out or recapture tax, like *Christine* in the first two examples. There is a trade-off, then, between explicitly targeting the poor and the incentive effects on work from doing so.

An across-the-board tax increase, as in the third example, can minimize the distortions to *Ava* and *Ben* that a more targeted approach creates. First, because additional revenue can be raised from individuals like *Christine*, the rate can be lower, creating fewer distortions. Second, it does not implicitly tax *Ava* and *Ben* more heavily than *Christine*, as the net effect of earning an additional dollar would now be the same for all three.

We can thus see that once funding mechanisms are taken into account, almost all UBI proposals vary with income. The only questions are how much, whether this variance is made explicit, and the extent to which disincentives are minimized.

In contrast, the only time a UBI is truly universal is if it is funded by a tax or fee on something that does not vary by income. For example, we could use revenue from auctioning off the broadband spectrum, and distribute the proceeds to all equally. Unless the true cost of such an auction fell harder on upper-income individuals, such a UBI would not vary by income and would be universal in the sense contemplated by Van Parijs and Vanderborght. One final caveat. It is important to emphasize that some types of funding—such as a carbon tax—may appear not to vary with income. But as carbon usage increases with income, paying for a UBI with a carbon tax still has the effect of at least loosely varying a UBI by income.

In most circumstances, therefore, a UBI varies with income even if it does not appear to do so at first glance. But why beat around the bush? Why bother sending checks to everyone if you're simply going to take it back in taxes? Doesn't a means-tested program make more sense? We turn to this question in the next chapter.

9

NO, REALLY, WHY ARE YOU SENDING A CHECK TO BILLIONAIRES LIKE JEFF BEZOS?

We just saw that explicitly phasing out or recapturing a UBI is mathematically equivalent to paying it to everybody and offsetting the cost with higher taxes elsewhere. Why might we choose one approach over the other?[1]

One consideration is administrative ease. As a practical matter, it is simpler to pay a UBI to all (likely via direct deposit), and integrate a surtax that offsets its cost into the existing tax system (a surtax is simply an additional tax that is added to something already being taxed). This avoids the need to track income throughout the year to adjust the size of your UBI payment each month. Instead, if you qualify based on citizenship status, you will be entitled to a transfer in the amount of the full UBI regardless of what you make. The government needs to collect income information only once a year, when you file your taxes—as is the case now. A key benefit of this arrangement is that it uses *ex post* information—how much income you had during the past year—to determine your offsetting tax liability for that past year, which in turn determines whether you benefit on net from the UBI.

Another way to take advantage of hindsight is to use last year's income to pay a means-tested UBI this year. The EITC and Child Tax Credit (CTC) work like this. But here's the catch—this can create a timing mismatch between past income and current needs. Consider the Covid-19 relief payments transferred to many Americans in the

Spring of 2020. The payments phased out with income, but one's income from either 2018 or 2019 was used to determine the size of the payment one received in 2020. For many individuals whose livelihoods were damaged in the pandemic, income from one or two years prior drastically understated their current needs and how much of a benefit they should qualify for based on their current year income.

So why not use more current income information, updated frequently, to adjust the size of one's UBI throughout the year? After all, that's what many existing welfare programs do. Well, measuring income and adjusting payment size more frequently is administratively cumbersome.

It's much simpler to pay one amount to all, and then impose a tax later. Compare someone who makes $30,000 per year with someone who makes $300,000 per year. Each would receive monthly checks in, say, 2022. When they go to file their taxes in 2023 for the year 2022, the lower-income person would not owe an additional surtax, whereas the upper-income person would. The system can look backwards and say "Gosh, you didn't need that money after all" to the higher earner.

That's the practical aspect. Politically, this arrangement has pros and cons. One advantage is that it portrays a UBI as a universal benefit, much like Social Security, Medicare, or public schools, rather than "welfare" that goes only to the poor. The downside, however, is that some members of the public may react negatively to the idea of wealthy individuals like Jeff Bezos receiving what appears to be a transfer, even if such individuals do not really benefit on net from the UBI. Financial journalist Felix Salmon reveals this misunderstanding, recently arguing that:

> UBI is a pretty inefficient way of giving poor people money. Think about it this way: Just 40% of a UBI's expenditure would go to the bottom 40% of the population, and a mere 10% would go to the 10% who need it most. What would happen to the rest of the money?
>
> Study after study has shown that when you give money to the homeless and the very poor, they don't spend it on frivolities like booze and tobacco: In fact, rates of drinking

and smoking invariably go down rather than up. On the other hand, if you gave *me* an extra $1,500 per month, no strings attached, I'm sure a significant chunk of that would end up in my wine fridge. That might be popular with my local wine merchants, but as a means of redistributing society's wealth in the interests of fairness and equality, it does leave something to be desired.[2]

Despite being a generally smart and perceptive commentator on economic policy, Salmon has been distracted by the word "universal." As we've seen, high-income individuals like himself would not actually be receiving extra funds from the government. In fact, they'd likely owe at least a few thousand dollars per year more in taxes if a UBI of any substantial size were implemented. Perhaps one way to counter the perception of the rich "receiving" a basic income would be to add an extra line to the individual income tax return that shows the additional surtax paid by a high-income individual that effectively recaptures their UBI.

Alternatively, a UBI could be cast as a new tax credit such as a "citizen's credit" or something along those lines, without changing its underlying nature. And even though tax credits have traditionally been paid out annually (as we'll discuss more in later chapters), it is possible to pay them more frequently. In this case, the difference between such a credit and a UBI would be merely semantic. Nevertheless, evidence suggests that the public is more favorably disposed to "tax credits" than to cash transfer spending programs. Future work can help illuminate whether and to what extent semantic framing would increase support.

10

WOULD A BASIC INCOME REPLACE EXISTING WELFARE POLICIES OR SUPPLEMENT THEM?

We've seen that the idea behind a UBI is that *everyone* receives an unconditional check from the government. But what about people who are already benefiting from government transfers—would a UBI replace or supplement existing welfare programs? To some, cost will be a defining factor in whether they support or oppose a UBI (we'll discuss this more in the next section). A UBI layered on top of existing programs will obviously cost more than one that replaces such benefits. But even ignoring costs, there are two schools of thought as to which is the ideal approach.

Most left-leaning UBI advocates start from the premise that justice requires much greater amounts of redistribution than most countries currently provide. Simply keeping citizens out of abject poverty or providing a basic safety net (as most current welfare programs do) is insufficient. Instead, all citizens should have more than enough to meet their basic needs. Indeed, the goal should be providing resources that are ample enough to ensure that we all enjoy some degree of "real" freedom in our lives—enough to say no to a miserable job, enough to leave an abusive spouse. A UBI that simply replaces existing welfare programs would fall far short on this view. Instead, a UBI should be layered atop existing welfare programs—an approach often referred to in the UBI literature as "UBI-plus."

In contrast, other proponents believe that a UBI should replace the existing welfare system but not expand it (an approach known as "UBI-minus"). Although not exclusively so, these advocates tend to be political conservatives or libertarians. Some supporters—such as libertarian economist Milton Friedman and conservative scholar Charles Murray—only begrudgingly accept governmental redistribution. Although they'd prefer a world with less redistribution than currently provided, they believe a UBI is the best means of redistribution if society is nevertheless going to insist upon it. Other conservatives and libertarians—such as the authors—believe both that society has (at minimum) a duty to provide a basic safety net to all and that a UBI is the best means of doing so.

Both types of replacement advocates, however, generally envision fairly low levels of redistribution that are in line with (or roughly in line with) what's currently provided. A UBI's raison d'etre is not to increase the quantity of governmental aid, but rather its quality. These advocates look at the current system and see an incoherent patchwork of inefficient, outdated, and paternalistic programs that disincentivize work. Replacing this mess with one streamlined cash program is the goal. Even so, however, questions will remain about which programs should be replaced. Cash transfers such as the EITC seem like easy cases. But what about school lunches—should families be given cash so that children can bring or purchase their own lunch, or might there be economies of scale or other efficiency reasons to continue providing in-kind lunches at school? Replacing versus supplementing might not be an all-or-nothing proposition.

Regardless, we think it likely that any proposal with a politically realistic chance of being implemented would be a UBI-minus that replaces at least some existing programs. (And although we try to distinguish between a UBI-plus and a UBI-minus where applicable throughout this book, readers can generally assume that we are referring to a UBI-minus when we don't distinguish.)

In practice, the extent to which a UBI-minus replaces current welfare programs will likely vary from jurisdiction to jurisdiction. Ignoring cost, some jurisdictions are more favorably disposed to large levels of redistribution than others. Some jurisdictions view health care and subsidized childcare as basic government services akin to the military that should be unaffected by a UBI, while others consider such programs to be the type of "welfare" that could be replaced.

And then there's cost, which we'll turn to next.

11

HOW MUCH WOULD A BASIC INCOME COST?

So, let's turn to the million (or trillion) dollar question—how much will a UBI cost?[1]

The short answer is somewhere between "not nothing" and "a lot," but precisely how much a UBI would cost depends on how big it is, how many people receive it, and what programs it replaces. As of 2021, the US population was roughly 335 million.[2] First consider a UBI-plus that supplements existing programs. A $500-per-month UBI paid to the full population would have a gross annual cost of $1.992 trillion; doubling that to a $1,000-per-month UBI-plus would cost twice that. A monthly UBI of $500 or $1,000 that included seniors but not children and teens would have a respective gross cost of $1.514 trillion or $3.029 trillion; including children but excluding seniors age 65 years and over would have a respective gross cost of $1.663 trillion or $3.326 trillion.[3] A UBI that excluded both groups would cost even less, $1.168 trillion and $2.335 trillion respectively. (Note that these figures include non-citizens, whose treatment we discuss in chapter 16. A UBI that excluded the roughly 25 million non-citizens[4] present in the United States would, of course, cost a bit less than one that included them.)

These numbers sound huge. But they are *gross* numbers, and represent the true price tag only if a UBI was layered entirely on top of existing welfare programs, without replacing a single one (the UBI-plus approach). As we just saw, some proponents advocate for this approach as a theoretical matter. Yet a $500- or $1,000-per-month UBI of this type would require trillions of dollars of new funding, almost certainly in the form of new taxes. As a practical matter, it is unlikely that voters in most jurisdictions would approve such a plan.

Most serious real-world policy proposals therefore envision that a UBI of this size would replace various cash or near-cash transfer programs (the UBI-minus approach). As a result, the *net* cost of a UBI would be lower. How much lower depends on what, exactly, is cut and whether an explicit phase-out or recapture tax is imposed.

Some UBI proponents (generally on the more conservative or libertarian end of the spectrum) believe that a UBI can be funded without across-the-board tax increases *entirely* by consolidating an array of existing programs. To illustrate, consider Charles Murray's plan, which would pay $13,000 per year to each adult in the United States. A surtax imposed on incomes between $30,000 and $60,000 would recapture up to half that amount for individuals with incomes over $30,000, but there would otherwise be no additional taxes. To fund this plan, Murray proposes cutting all federal transfer payments to individuals. This includes programs that are obviously transfers, such as SNAP, Social Security, unemployment insurance, the Children's Health Insurance Program (CHIP), Temporary Assistance to Needy Families (TANF), Medicare and Medicaid, the Affordable Care Act (ACA) premium assistance program, school lunches, Pell grants, federal housing assistance, the EITC, and the refundable portion of the Child Tax Credit (CTC). It would also include programs such as the low-income home energy assistance program, the black lung benefit program, and the September 11th victim compensation fund. Murray would also cut federal programs that favor specific groups and industries, such as agricultural and farm subsidies.[5]

Murray's proposal is audacious in that it proposes cutting Medicare, Medicaid, and Social Security while requiring individuals to fund their own health care and retirement. While some might applaud this belt-tightening, we suspect that such a plan would have little chance of passing—just like any plan that imposed massive taxes to fund a UBI that supplemented existing programs without replacing any of them.

The most likely course is somewhere in the middle. Most proposals—such as Stern's and Yang's in the United States—suggest consolidating "welfare programs," but they often don't specify exactly which programs they are counting as welfare programs. (Stern, for example, doesn't list the "126 welfare programs that currently cost $1 trillion a year"[6] that his plan would cut.) Presumably, these proposals mean programs such as TANF, Social Security, SNAP, the Women, Infants and Children (WIC) nutritional aid program, Section 8 housing assistance vouchers, the EITC, and the CTC in the United States, and their counterparts elsewhere. Medicare, Medicaid, and Social Security are generally left untouched, although some plans suggest cutting Social Security for future beneficiaries.

One hiccup of this approach is that any restructuring of aid programs will inevitably leave some citizens worse off (and others better off), and a UBI that renders many current aid beneficiaries worse off than they are now would likely have little political support. To that end, some UBI advocates—such as 2020 presidential candidate Andrew Yang—have proposed giving citizens a choice between keeping their existing benefits and receiving a UBI. Whether a UBI would make some citizens worse off is discussed in more detail in chapter 53.

Many plans also propose cutting what are known as "tax expenditures," which are deductions and credits that provide benefits to taxpayers who engage in certain activities. (Think of the electric vehicle tax credit. If the government lowers your taxes by $7,500 because you buy an electric car, you have $7,500 more in your pocket and the government has $7,500 less in its pocket—just as if it gave you $7,500 directly.) Common tax expenditures on the chopping block of many proposals are the mortgage interest deduction, tax-exempt bond interest, the charitable deduction, the deduction for state and local taxes, and the exclusion of employer contributions to health insurance.

So, once you account for eliminating existing welfare programs and most tax expenditures, what would the net cost of a UBI be? Using 2021 estimates, cutting SNAP ($135 billion), TANF ($35 billion), WIC ($5 billion), unemployment insurance ($37 billion), and Section 8 ($33 billion) yields a total of $225 billion. Eliminating the EITC and the child tax credit yields almost $200 billion (using 2018 data). Cutting common tax expenditures such as the home mortgage deduction, the qualified small business deduction, stepped-up basis, the charitable deduction, and the exclusion of employer-provided health insurance would yield another $335 million or so. Eliminating the tax-favored status of Social Security Old Age and Survivor's

Insurance (OASI) benefits and trimming but not eliminating two additional programs run by the Social Security Administration—Social Security Disability Insurance (SSDI) and Supplemental Security Income (SSI)—contributes roughly another $94 billion, as we discuss in chapter 15. Together, these savings would reduce the net cost of a UBI by roughly $854 billion.

This still leaves a net cost in the billions—or even trillions—of dollars, depending on the size of the UBI and the number of people to whom it's provided. For example, a $500-per-month UBI to all US residents would still have a net cost of $1.138 trillion. The next section discusses where these funds might come from.

12

HOW COULD A BASIC INCOME BE FUNDED?

As we've seen, most serious UBI proposals would require substantial new revenue to implement, even after eliminating other costly programs. Where would this money come from? Taxes. On what? Once again, that depends.

Any substantial UBI—say $500 or $1,000 per month—would require additional taxes on income or consumption. One of the most popular funding proposals in the United States is a value-added tax (VAT), with which readers elsewhere are likely already familiar. (At least 160 other countries already have a VAT or similar.) A VAT is a tax on consumption—similar to a sales tax, although it is collected at many points throughout the production and sales process instead of solely at the end (as US sales taxes are). Yang, for example, proposes a 10% VAT (which the Tax Foundation estimates would raise $952 billion);[1] Stern proposes a VAT of "5 to 10 percent," which he estimates would raise somewhere between $650 billion and $1.3 trillion.[2]

Other advocates believe the simplest way to raise comparable sums is to build on what we already have—that is, the existing US income tax system—instead of creating a new system that is unfamiliar to the US public. For example, one of the authors has proposed a surtax of just over 7% on non-UBI income to raise an estimated $943 billion to help fund a $500-per-month UBI.[3] Relatedly, many commentators propose additional changes to the income tax system, such as removing the lower preferential rates for capital gains (Stern and Hughes are in this camp).

Although a VAT or surtax on income are the most likely vehicles to raise substantial additional revenues, many UBI plans rely on other types of taxes as well. In some plans, these taxes supplement new or increased income or consumption taxes and/or each other. In others, they are the sole source of funding. Realistically, however, any UBI financed by only one or a few of the following would not be very large.

One such tax is a financial transactions tax (FTT) or "Robin Hood" tax, which is a tax imposed on both the buyer and seller of specified financial instruments such as stocks, bonds, and derivatives. As of 2021, ten European countries had FTTs of varying sizes, including France, Switzerland, Italy, Belgium, Spain, Finland, and the United Kingdom. Interest in an FTT is growing in the United States as well, and both Stern and Yang propose using an FTT to partially fund their UBIs. Stern proposes a 0.25% tax on stock trades that he estimates would raise over $150 billion.[4] Yang suggests a 0.1% tax; revenue estimates of this proposal range from $50 billion by Yang's campaign to $78 billion by the Tax Foundation.

Yang's plan also includes a second common suggestion, a carbon tax.[5] Interestingly, several prominent Republicans have recently proposed taxing carbon while issuing consumers a "carbon dividend" that is essentially a small UBI. Revenue estimates from potential carbon taxes vary. One of us has estimated elsewhere that holding emissions constant, a $36 tax per metric ton would yield roughly $190 billion per year;[6] the Tax Foundation estimates that Yang's proposed tax of $40 per metric ton would raise $123 billion.

A third alternative is a wealth tax, recently popularized in the United States by then-presidential candidate Elizabeth Warren and academic Thomas Piketty. Wealth taxes are imposed on the value of all your assets—think of them like a property tax, but on everything, not just your home. The United States does not have a national wealth tax; experience elsewhere, such as in Europe, has been mixed due to administrative difficulties. Stern proposes a 1.5% tax on personal assets whose total value exceeds a $1,000,000 exemption amount. Notably, this is a much lower exemption amount than proposed by Senators Elizabeth Warren ($50,000,000) and Bernie Sanders ($32,000,000).

The taxes just discussed—on consumption, income, financial transactions, carbon, and wealth—are the most commonly proposed, and have already been tried and tested. Two novel ideas include taxing data and using proceeds from auctioning the broadband spectrum;[7] advocates of these ideas argue that such resources belong to us all and therefore their fruits should be returned to us in the form of a UBI.

And a final idea—the land value tax or single tax popularized by Henry George—has a long academic history, but little real-world experience. A land value tax operates much like today's property taxes, but ignores the value of improvements such as houses, factories, and other buildings. Many UBI proponents favor using such taxes on the theory that land itself should be considered a commonly-owned resource whose value should be shared among us—see chapter 63 for a discussion. Although this type of tax is quite popular with many UBI advocates, the public lacks familiarity with it and we suspect such a tax is unlikely to be implemented.

13

WOULD A BASIC INCOME BE PAID TO INDIVIDUALS OR HOUSEHOLDS?

Would a UBI be paid to individuals, or to households?[1] Most proposals view a UBI as an individual entitlement. For example, a husband and wife would each receive his or her own separate UBI. This might seem like a merely cosmetic distinction, but it's not. Consider the various rationales for a UBI. A key justification is respecting the dignity and autonomy of each member of a community; separately delivering the UBI to each eligible individual reflects this. It provides each individual with at least some ability to make financial decisions free of others, gives household members more of an equal say in finances, and makes it easier for those in abusive relationships to leave. In contrast, a household benefit would require you to make decisions jointly with others, which compromises your freedom and the ability to say "no."

A separate, but related, question is whether the grant's size should vary based on household composition. For example, most current welfare programs provide married or co-habitating individuals with somewhat less than a single individual. The maximum monthly SNAP benefit for a one-person household is $250, while the maximum for a two-person household is $459.[2] The leading UBI proposals are mixed. Many, such as Murray and Stern, do not vary by household size, whereas Chris Hughes suggests that household composition should influence size and/or eligibility.

Why might the UBI adjust for household size? Well, it costs more to meet one's basic needs living alone than in a household of two or more persons. Consider all the economies of scale that come from having a roommate or spouse. It generally doesn't cost twice as much to feed two people instead of one. Two people can share one refrigerator. The electricity bill for two people is likely not double that for one person. And so on. Reflecting this, studies of income inequality and poverty generally use equivalence scales to estimate the relative costs of households of various sizes. One common scale reflects an assumption that the cost of living for two people is 1.41 times the cost of living for one person. If the cost of living for a single individual was $1,000, then a budget of $1,410 (or roughly $700 per person) would cover a two-person household—meaning that doubling up saves approximately 30%.[3]

However, there are several compelling counter-arguments. Most importantly, adjusting for household size interferes with decisions to marry and cohabitate—a common critique of many existing welfare schemes. To illustrate, imagine a UBI in which single individuals receive $12,000 per year, while married or cohabitating couples together receive UBIs that total only $18,000. Such a structure creates an overall penalty of $6,000 for childless adults who decide to marry or cohabitate. Living separately, the couple nets $24,000 (two UBIs of $12,000 each); together, they net $18,000. Most would agree that governmental policy should not *discourage* marriage or the formation of two-person households, regardless of whether one prefers governmental neutrality or a positive bias toward marriage.

Administrative concerns also counsel against adjusting for household size. As implied above, neutrality and consistency suggest treating marital and other cohabitation arrangements similarly. Yet living arrangements are often transitory, especially for low-income individuals for whom housing instability is an unfortunate fact of life. Relatives, roommates, and romantic partners frequently yet irregularly move in and out. Adjusting the size of someone's UBI to reflect these frequent changes would significantly burden individuals and administrative agencies. And beyond these costs, adjusting a UBI for household size would make it harder for low-income individuals to plan for the future. Indeed, the fact that a UBI provides a predictable benefit that does not vary in size for a given individual is one key advantage of a UBI over existing welfare programs, where beneficiaries must often adjust to changes in the size of their benefits.

14

WOULD CHILDREN RECEIVE A BASIC INCOME?

If the UBI is an individual benefit, does that mean children would receive a UBI too?[1] After all, children have long been viewed as among the most deserving recipients of governmental and philanthropic aid, and few would dispute that child poverty is a problem worthy of attention. Reflecting this, most current welfare programs favor families with children—witness the minimal aid provided to childless adults by the EITC in the United States, and the proliferation of universal child allowances globally.

Yet existing proposals are surprisingly divided on this point. Charles Murray, Andy Stern, Chris Hughes, and former presidential candidate Andrew Yang would exclude children altogether from their UBIs. In contrast, basic income advocate Scott Santens would include children, but at a lower rate—an approach also taken by the ultimately unsuccessful Swiss referendum in 2016. In contrast, one of us has argued elsewhere that children should be included on the same terms as adults.[2]

So, what are the pros and cons of including children?[3] The most frequent objections are administrative in nature. As Stern writes: "[J]ust think of all the issues that come up when you try to get your mind around giving [a basic income] to a ten-year-old."[4] It is true that a ten-year-old hoarding hundreds of dollars in her piggy bank or managing a large savings account seems fantastical, as is the notion that a ten-year-old would spend hundreds of dollars a month wisely. Yet, as is the case with existing social benefits geared toward children, the UBI would almost certainly be paid to the child's parent or guardian. Alaska does precisely this, paying a child's Permanent Fund Dividend to a designated adult on her behalf.

This brings up two related questions. First, what of the risk that negligent parents will squander their child's UBI? One option would be to pay a child's UBI to a trust fund on her behalf (somewhat like a Baby Bond; see chapter 30). But this precludes the funds from currently benefiting the child, undercutting many of the welfare gains that are associated with providing cash to families with children (see chapters 28 and 51). Perhaps because these gains outweigh the risk that parents will waste a child's UBI (which we address in more depth in chapter 52), a UBI that included children most likely would not require use of a trust or similar account.

Second, questions will occasionally arise as to which adult should receive the UBI on behalf of the child—as is already the case with child allowances around the world and with benefits such as the child tax credit and the EITC in the United States.[5] And although no program has crafted a perfect solution, the problem of matching children to guardians in the face of uncertainty doesn't paralyze existing child allowances. Moreover, in some countries such as the United States, the myriad programs that deliver benefits to families with children use differing eligibility requirements for matching children to parents. This is true even for the various credits and benefits located within the US tax code! Replacing these various programs with one UBI will not eliminate child attribution questions, but it will streamline those determinations and reduce the complexity associated with having to deal with multiple differing eligibility determinations at once.

Murray raises an additional, substantive objection—he argues that including children in a UBI scheme would encourage low-income adults to have more children.[6] Empirical evidence on this point is mixed.[7] Yet even if we assume that including children would encourage lower-income adults to bear more children, it is not clear what to make of that. Some might argue that financial constraints shouldn't limit such an important life decision; others might counter that financial constraints limit all sorts of crucial life choices, and that family size should not be singled out. Some might think that encouraging fertility to ward off decreasing birth rates is a beneficial social policy; others might argue that the state should be neutral in such matters.

The strongest argument for including children is that doing so would alleviate child poverty and help children. As discussed in chapters 28 and 44, cash and near-cash transfers are associated with numerous benefits for children, such as increased educational attainment, higher test scores, fewer disciplinary actions, better nutrition, and improvements in emotional and behavioral health. This argument is especially forceful if a UBI would replace existing cash and near-cash programs. In that case, a UBI that excluded children would exacerbate the problem of child poverty.

15

WOULD SENIORS RECEIVE A BASIC INCOME ON TOP OF SOCIAL SECURITY BENEFITS?

That's children. What about seniors?[1] Whether they'd receive a UBI in addition to governmental pensions such as Social Security is an especially devilish detail.[2] On one hand, such pensions already serve as a proto-UBI for seniors; one might wonder why seniors should receive essentially two UBIs instead of one. Reflecting this intuition, the Earned Income Tax Credit (EITC; the existing cash transfer program most similar to a UBI) already excludes seniors without qualifying child dependents. Moreover, such benefits are expensive. In 2020, the Social Security program for retirees, Old Age and Survivor's Insurance (OASI), cost the US government over $950 billion.[3] Eliminating OASI would go a long way toward funding a UBI that included seniors.

This question is moot for those who believe that a UBI-plus should add to, not replace, existing benefits. But for proponents who argue that a UBI-minus should replace existing welfare-type programs (including other age-specific benefits like child credits), why should seniors be treated more favorably than other groups? A few plausible responses spring to mind. First, as of January 2022, the average monthly OASI payment for retirees was $1,614 per month.[4] Replacing these payments with a UBI of $1,000 or $500 per month would leave millions of seniors worse off, especially if other programs upon which less-fortunate seniors rely (such as SNAP) were also eliminated. Some UBI advocates—such as Murray—have thus proposed allowing seniors to choose between OASI benefits and a UBI.

Even though it would not offset a substantial portion of a UBI's cost, requiring seniors to choose would still help close the funding gap somewhat. However, this could run into some political objections. Many consider OASI benefits to be something they have already "paid for," given that (1) OASI is funded through a separate tax on wages and (2) benefits are determined in part by past wages and past tax payments. This leads many people (incorrectly) to view their tax payments during their working years as directly funding their later OASI benefits, much like contributions to a 401(k) plan directly fund later payments from that plan.

Seniors who view OASI through this lens would likely feel as if they are being forced to choose between something others receive automatically (regardless of other income) and an income source they've already paid for. They might note that individuals who receive private pensions or annuities are not forced to choose. Conditioning receipt of the UBI upon giving up one's OASI benefits, on this account, effectively imposes a much higher marginal tax rate on OASI benefits than other income. Given that Social Security is the "third rail" of American politics,[5] pitching a UBI as an outright replacement for or competitor to OASI will likely make it more difficult to pass politically.

To that end, one of us has elsewhere suggested another compromise that minimizes the costs of including seniors in a UBI without forcing them to give up OASI benefits.[6] First, OASI benefits are currently untaxed for a majority of OASI beneficiaries.[7] Ending this favored status would treat them comparably to other income streams and save around $27.2 billion per year that could help pay for a UBI. Second, we proposed reducing benefit amounts by one-third (admittedly an arbitrary number) for Social Security Disability Insurance (SSDI) and Supplemental Security Income (SSI), both of which are also administered by the Social Security Administration. This would save an additional $66.63 billion.[8] Although these changes would save a total of $93.8 billion, they do not come close to offsetting the cost of extending even a $500-per-month UBI to the 57 million senior Americans. Moreover, even these changes are still vulnerable to the same political considerations that arise any time Social Security reforms are discussed. The question of seniors will remain especially devilish.

16

WOULD IMMIGRANTS AND NONCITIZENS RECEIVE A BASIC INCOME?

Another controversial decision is whether immigrants would receive a UBI. And again, we see that it depends on whom you are asking! The default seems to be that a UBI would be limited to citizens; as Van Parijs and Vanderborght note, common program names such as a "citizen's income" and a "citizen's wage" reflect this assumption. Most UBI proposals in the United States—such as Murray's and Stern's—limit them to citizens without discussion, though of course a polity could decide otherwise and extend a UBI to noncitizen residents, or even non-residents.

Before getting into the pros and cons of including immigrants, note that by its very nature, this question assumes that a UBI would *not* be global in nature (see chapter 18). Most serious UBI proposals envision its implementation at a national level, although there are UBI advocates who urge a global reach. Some argue that the demands of justice do not stop at national borders; others assert that a global UBI is required to address the problems mentioned below related to selective immigration and emigration. Whatever the merits of these views, it is highly unlikely a global UBI would be implemented in the foreseeable future. Most advocates therefore push for either a national UBI or, somewhat more broadly, one encompassing all the member states of an economic association such as the European Union. And of course, smaller jurisdictions—like individual states or cities—might decide to offer their own UBIs. In fact, as chapter 36 explores, American cities like Chicago and Oakland have already begun UBI experiments.

Assuming a national UBI, pragmatism and theory collide on the question of extending a UBI to new arrivals.[1] Many theoretical justifications for a UBI counsel treating all residents equally, whether they are citizens or not. Immigrants, like all people, deserve to live with dignity and respect, and those who are concerned with alleviating poverty and suffering generally would have little reason to distinguish between citizens and noncitizens. It is generally within a polity's interest to provide immigrants with equal opportunities to develop their skills and contribute to society. On the other hand, those who conceive of a UBI as a means of creating buy-in for the social order from the less-advantaged might not see the need to get the buy-in of those who arrive after the social order is established.

In contrast, most pragmatic considerations weigh in favor of limiting a UBI's scope. First, extending a UBI to all immigrants immediately upon arrival could theoretically encourage illegal immigration, although empirical evidence on the influence of welfare benefits and migration levels is mixed.[2] Doing so could also complicate discussions about the ideal level of immigration, as it would increase the cost of welcoming immigrants and potentially change who desires to immigrate by making immigration more attractive to lower-skilled or less-motivated individuals. Immediately granting a UBI to new arrivals would also increase the cost of a UBI, potentially damaging its political support. Relatedly, the more expensive a UBI, the greater chance that businesses and individuals will relocate elsewhere to minimize taxes.

Likely reflecting these concerns, most cash and near-cash assistance programs in the United States restrict access in some ways. Almost all—including SNAP, Medicaid, SSDI, and SSI[3]—exclude undocumented adults. The treatment of documented adults is mixed. Programs such as SNAP, Medicaid, and SSI impose years-long length-of-residency requirements,[4] while lawful immigrants with taxpayer identification numbers are eligible for tax benefits such as the EITC and CTC either immediately or within a year.[5] In-kind benefits, especially for children, tend to have looser eligibility requirements; undocumented children may attend public schools and are eligible for Head Start, the National School Lunch Program, SNAP, and WIC. And emergency medical care is available to all regardless of immigration status.

Two compromises seem most likely. The first is a waiting period. Brazil's *Bolsa Familia* program (which shared many characteristics of a UBI) took this approach, requiring five years of residency.[6] Alaska has a similar approach regarding its dividend program (discussed in chapter 32). It requires individuals to (1) reside in Alaska for the full calendar year before the year for which they are claiming a dividend; (2) have the intent to remain indefinitely; and (3) not claim residency in or accept the benefits of residency in another state.[7]

A second resolution might be to include lawful permanent residents in a UBI while excluding other noncitizens. Limiting a UBI to individuals who have lawful status shouldn't unduly encourage individuals to enter a country illegally or overstay a visa; and the requirements for obtaining permanent residency could dissuade those who worry that extending a UBI to newcomers would change the mix of new arrivals to a polity.

What to do about immigrants raises another question—what about citizens living abroad or who have extended periods away from a jurisdiction? It seems plausible to exclude citizens living abroad, especially if they are eligible for substantial benefits in their new countries of residence. Layering a UBI on top of that would amount to a sort of "double payment." Of course, this requires determining who is and is not living abroad. Again, Alaska might provide a model. To be eligible for a dividend, residents generally cannot be away from Alaska for more than 180 days in a given year,[8] and at no time can they establish or intend to establish permanent residence elsewhere.[9]

17

WOULD A BASIC INCOME BE ADJUSTED FOR REGIONAL DIFFERENCES IN COST OF LIVING?

In the last chapter, we noted that a UBI would most likely be instituted on a national level. How would a UBI address intra-national cost-of-living differences? Would citizens living in higher-cost areas receive a larger UBI than citizens living in lower-cost ones?[1]

By now, the answer shouldn't surprise you—it depends on who you ask! Existing UBI-like programs, such as Alaska's Permanent Fund Dividend, do not account for cost-of-living variations within Alaska; the Finland experiment also provided the same size grant regardless of the participant's location. Likewise, most of the more well-known UBI proposals do not vary by size within a given polity, although some do (such as Facebook co-founder Chris Hughes's pseudo-UBI proposal).

The strongest argument for providing a larger UBI to individuals living in high-cost areas is that such individuals require greater resources to meet their basic needs. For example, the Massachusetts Institute of Technology's Living Wage calculator estimates that in 2022, a single adult in San Francisco County needed over $58,000 to cover basic expenses such as housing, food, medical care, transportation, and taxes.[2] In contrast, a single adult in Marion County, Indiana (which includes Indianapolis), could scrape by on just over half that amount, or roughly $29,000.[3]

Supporting this intuition, some federal benefits in the United States—such as Section 8 housing vouchers and the Affordable Care

Act premium tax credit—vary by location; the federal government's pay scale does as well. On the other hand, the Internal Revenue Code generally ignores a taxpayer's location. The rate schedules and the standard deduction (which shields roughly the first $13,000 of a taxpayer's income from tax) do not vary by location; neither do the EITC and the CTC.

To many, whether these differences should matter will turn on whether one's location is considered a choice. It is a commonly held moral belief that people are responsible for their choices, and should in most cases bear the costs of them. Compare *Alice*, who values mild winters and loves long walks along the beach, with *Bob*, who doesn't care where he lives, but really, really enjoys dining on steak and lobster. Few would argue that *Bob*'s preference for luxurious foods merits a larger UBI. But what about *Alice*'s desire to live in California—is that also a preference for a luxury good that should be treated like *Bob*'s taste for lobster (in other words, ignored)?

Or should where one lives be considered a factor beyond one's control? The average American of any age lives only eighteen miles from her mother;[4] and the average 25–35 year old lives only five miles from a parent or in-law.[5] Interstate migration has been declining for several decades; early estimates show the pandemic did not reverse this trend.[6] This suggests that location is largely a function of birthplace and family ties—that is, a chance event that raises the amount of income that individuals born in expensive locations need in order to function as an equal citizen and ensure their basic needs are met. On this view, individuals unlucky enough to be born into high-cost areas like San Francisco might have a claim to a larger UBI that does not depend on subsidizing expensive choices. On the other hand, it is plausible that a UBI would make moving easier by helping individuals afford moving costs and any increased expenses for child and eldercare that might come with living further from one's family.

Moreover, treating where one lives as a matter of chance does not necessarily lead to the conclusion that people in more expensive areas should receive a larger UBI. Although such areas have higher costs, they also tend to have higher wages and more employment opportunities.[7] Is a San Francisco Bay Area native unlucky, because she was born in a high cost-of-living area? Or lucky, because she was born in an area with an unemployment rate that is almost 20%

lower than the national average and average weekly wages that are roughly 45% higher than the national average?[8]

These questions illustrate a dilemma. Even if we did want to implement cost-of-living adjustments, whom should we target? People who live in areas with high wages and a high cost of living, or people who live in areas with low wages and a low cost of living? We can see that even if such adjustments are attractive in theory, they are difficult to implement in practice.[9] Add in the likely administrative costs of adjusting for location, and we can see why most plans eschew such adjustments.

18

WHAT'S THE BEST LEVEL TO IMPLEMENT A BASIC INCOME—A COUNTRY? A CITY? GLOBALLY?

Our discussion so far has proceeded on the assumption that a UBI would be adopted at a national level, and most serious policy proposals share that assumption. But a national UBI isn't the only option available to UBI advocates. In a federal system like the United States, a UBI could be implemented by a state. A UBI could even be implemented by a city—a possibility highlighted by recent pilot programs in the United States (see chapter 36). Alternatively, moving up in scale rather than down, a UBI could conceivably be implemented on a global scale. This chapter will discuss some of the advantages and disadvantages associated with each of these options.

National

The national level is the default level for major social legislation. National budgets are generally far larger than state and local budgets, which is important for potentially expensive programs like health care, retirement insurance, or a guaranteed income. And legislation enacted at the national level has, of course, a far broader reach. To the extent that social welfare programs like a UBI are grounded on arguments about the basic rights of citizens, it seems appropriate that the legislation should apply to *all* citizens, not just some.

But national legislation has its drawbacks, too. As we have seen, there are many different ways that a UBI could be designed. Within a nation, however, there is only one national government, while there are often many smaller jurisdictions. One advantage of federalism, or decentralization, is that it allows different jurisdictions to try different approaches. Smaller jurisdictions can learn from the experience of their neighbors, and have an incentive to design better policies in order to attract people and businesses to their state. National legislation, on the other hand, tends to be very difficult to change once it has been enacted due to the powerful interest groups it creates (see chapter 53) and the lack of easy "exit" options for those dissatisfied with the nation's approach.

The issue of immigration also poses a challenge for a UBI set at the national level—see chapters 16 and 54 for a more complete discussion. Briefly, the problem is that nations that adopt a UBI for all citizens or residents will tend to attract immigrants seeking to benefit from that UBI. This will potentially increase the cost of a UBI greatly, unless measures are taken either to restrict immigration or to restrict the eligibility of immigrants for the UBI. Moreover, the mere *perception* that immigrants are benefitting from a UBI might also increase opposition to immigration in general.

The problem here is especially pressing for UBI advocates committed to social justice. Suppose a UBI is established in a relatively wealthy country like the United States, and that this leads the United States to adopt a more restrictive immigration policy. Under such a scenario, the poor in the United States might very well be better off than they would be without a UBI. But the *global* poor—the poor who are, by most objective standards, much worse off than the poor within the United States—might very well be worse off by virtue of being denied the opportunity to move to a wealthier country where jobs and other opportunities are more readily available. One might therefore object that a UBI in a wealthy country benefits the already relatively wealthy at the expense of the truly poor.

Cities and States

Enacting UBIs at the level of the city or state thus allows different jurisdictions to experiment with different approaches to policy design. But while there are certain advantages to this approach in terms of learning and adaptation, there may be important disadvantages as well.

For instance, the "competition" that ensues between states or cities might wind up being destructive rather than beneficial in its effect. Cities and states that offer a generous UBI will tend to have higher taxes than other jurisdictions. This will make them less attractive to businesses or residents, depending on who bears the burden of those taxes. Higher levels of benefits will also make those jurisdictions *more* attractive to low-income people who expect to be net beneficiaries of a UBI. A generous UBI will thus tend to drive wealth out, and to draw poverty in. Rather than competing to provide the *most* generous UBI, then, there is some reason to think that states and cities might actually compete to offer the *least* generous package—that a "race to the bottom" will ensue.

This creates a problem that parallels that of international migration, discussed above. But since migrating between cities and states *within* a nation is usually easier than migrating *between* nations, the problems posed by such migration will generally be even greater when UBIs are implemented at the sub-national level.

Global

From a purely theoretical perspective, a global UBI might make more sense than either a national or a sub-national UBI. Most arguments for the UBI, for instance, are *universal* in nature. That is, they are based on the dignity and worth of the person, or on the idea that natural resources belong to humanity as a whole. It is difficult to reconcile these arguments with a situation in which some people receive a UBI and others do not, simply by virtue of being born in one country rather than another.

A global UBI would also eliminate worries about migration and a race to the bottom. If all persons everywhere are covered equally by a UBI, this does not produce any perverse incentives for migration or for the closing of borders.

But a global UBI would pose unique challenges of its own. Some of these challenges have to do with the design of the policy. Questions like whether the UBI would vary with differences in regional cost of living (see chapter 17), or how it would be delivered (see chapter 23), are difficult enough to address at the national level, and far more challenging at the global level. Would a farmer in Indonesia be given the same amount as a taxi driver in New York? An amount sufficient to cover the basic needs of the former would be much lower than that necessary to meet the needs of the latter. On the other hand, if they *aren't* given the same amount, this might again produce incentives for people to move from low-cost to high-cost areas, raising problems about immigration all over again.

And, of course, even if a global UBI were desirable, it is far from clear just how we would go about establishing one. There is no global government, nor any global system of taxation. And the prospects of securing the agreement necessary to establish a UBI by means of an international treaty seem slim indeed. For the foreseeable future, then, a global UBI is an interesting thought experiment, and perhaps an admirable long-term aspiration. But that is as far as it goes.

19

WOULD A BASIC INCOME BE SUBJECT TO ASSET OR WEALTH TESTS?

We've already talked about how higher-income people most likely would not, on net, benefit from a UBI. But how would wealth (as opposed to income) affect one's UBI?[1] If the goal is to benefit the less well-off, or to redistribute from the haves to the have-nots, then shouldn't a UBI depend, at least in part, on the value of all one's wealth and assets? Compare *Alex* and *Beatrice*, who each have incomes of $5,000 per year. If *Alex* also has $10,000 sitting in the bank, while *Beatrice's* account is bare, then isn't *Alex* more capable of fending for himself and therefore less in need of a UBI?

Under this reasoning, several traditional aid programs in the United States—including SNAP, SSI, TANF, and the EITC—contain what are known as "asset tests." Briefly, if the value of a beneficiary's assets (or, in the case of the EITC, income from investment assets) exceeds a certain level, he or she is no longer eligible for benefits. What counts as an asset varies from program to program. Cash, bank account balances, and investment assets are always counted, while the precise treatment of cars and household goods varies somewhat.

While factoring in wealth might seem like a valid indicator of need, it presents several practical and behavioral complications. One is administrative. Most countries already have well-developed systems for measuring and reporting income. Often, these rely on third parties—for example, employers verify employee-reported wage income. In contrast, our technologies for valuing and reporting household assets and wealth are much less sophisticated. Individuals would be saddled with having to value and report their assets regularly; verifying these reports would increase burdens on the government, and there is often no obvious third party who can easily verify such information. A second practical complication is liquidity. Illiquid assets often do relatively little in the short term to improve an individual's ability to afford her basic needs.

You might wonder, can't these concerns be addressed by counting only liquid assets that are easily valued (such as cash, checking and savings accounts, and stocks and bonds traded on active markets)? Well, this would just incentivize people to hold their wealth in less liquid forms, such as insurance policies and gold bars. Anecdotally, some welfare recipients report buying more household durables such as furniture (which is not counted as an asset for most existing welfare program eligibility cut-offs) for this very reason.[2] Some low-income individuals who desire to save might start stockpiling cash, and forgo using banks entirely, if they knew that bank account balances would count against them for purposes of determining UBI eligibility. This incentive would only magnify the burdens that lower-income individuals already face in obtaining traditional financial services.

Thinking about behavioral responses illustrates another complication from considering wealth—an asset test would distort the choice between spending more now and saving for the future, likely decreasing incentives to save. Consider a UBI of $500 per month which decreases by 10 cents for each dollar of assets over $2,000. If *Beatrice*'s assets remain under $2,000, she receives the full amount. But if she manages to save some money and her wealth increases to $2,100, then her UBI decreases by $10 to $490 per month. She might well wonder, why bother to save? Cliff-like limits that render individuals totally ineligible for any benefit once assets exceed a set sum are even worse. They impose, in effect, wealth taxes that exceed 100%. Consider SNAP benefits. If a family's "countable assets" such as cash and bank accounts exceed $2,500, then the family loses *all* of its benefits. All of them! This cliff effect means that a few dollars of increased savings can cause a family to lose hundreds of dollars of monthly benefits.

This feels backwards to many people. Society arguably has an interest in encouraging savings among low-income households so that they can weather shocks such as a car breakdown or an unexpected medical bill. It is hard to see a reason why society should effectively discourage low-income households from accumulating savings.[3]

A final complication is that for poor individuals and households, asset levels often fluctuate dramatically. Someone's checking account might increase temporarily when a landlord repays a security deposit, or because of a tax refund, a one-time bonus, or a student loan payment. Low-income individuals and households often spend this money quickly to repay debts or purchase durables. As a result, allowing temporary infusions of cash to affect the size of someone's UBI could cause a reduction in her UBI that is unrelated to any real change in her needs. This "churn" in eligibility may in turn interfere with her ability to plan, which is one promised benefit of a UBI.

20

WILL PEOPLE BE ABLE TO SELL OR BORROW AGAINST THEIR BASIC INCOME?

Another question people often wonder about is whether beneficiaries would be able to sell their future UBI benefits for an immediate lump sum payment or use them as collateral for a loan.[1] This would essentially allow individuals to convert a UBI into something similar to the stakeholder grants suggested by Ackerman and Alstott.[2] As discussed in chapter 30, these are economically equivalent transactions. Nonetheless, most proposals—including Yang's Freedom Dividend—prohibit beneficiaries from selling or assigning their UBIs.[3]

Yet policy considerations point in competing directions. Consider *Anna*, who faces a sudden and unexpected large medical bill, and has only a few dollars in her bank account and no credit cards. Should she be able to borrow several thousand dollars today to cover the bill, assigning her next couple of years' worth of UBI payments to the lender as collateral?[4] Most people would probably support *Anna* borrowing from her UBI in order to meet a genuinely urgent need. But while *Anna* seems like an easy case, imagine *Bonnie*. In her early 20s, *Bonnie* sells her entire UBI in exchange for a lump sum payment that she squanders, and can't make ends meet for most of her adult life.

Whether you think the opportunities for *Anna* outweigh the danger to *Bonnie* or vice versa likely turns on why you support a UBI in the first instance. If you view the purpose of a UBI as enhancing freedom and opportunities for all, you probably support giving *Anna* this option. Allowing beneficiaries to assign or sell their UBI could expand access to credit for millions, who could then use the large lump sum payment to start a business, pay for college, or avert a financial catastrophe.

The principles of autonomy and respect also tend to weigh in favor of allowing assignability. Indeed, prohibiting beneficiaries from assigning their UBIs reproduces some of the same paternalism that UBI supporters often decry as a flaw of our current welfare state. Why should society favor saving over borrowing, when each can be a prudent financial decision depending on the circumstances?

Leaving these decisions to individuals signals that individuals are trusted to best know their own financial needs and to weigh the risks that come with cashing out one's UBI. The risk of someone later regretting a decision to convert their UBI to a lump sum is unfortunate, but the price of autonomy is bearing responsibility for one's own decisions.[5] If the goal is to increase financial opportunities for all Americans and then to let them chart their own course through life, then free assignability would seem to be the better approach.

Additionally, a practical benefit is that this could significantly lower borrowing costs for many low-income people, especially compared to the traditional options available to them such as payday loans or carrying large balances on high-interest credit cards. Presumably, lenders would offer lower rates on loans guaranteed by a UBI due to the additional security, although beneficiaries would of course be able to use their UBIs to make loan payments whether or not they are formally assignable. And if the government effectively controls the collateral for these loans, it might be easier to regulate against predatory lending.

If, however, one's goal is to ensure a subsistence-level income for all, then a freely assignable UBI will not accomplish that end. As much as we wish it were otherwise, there will be individuals who will squander away a lump sum. For this reason, Van Parijs and Vanderborght argue that beneficiaries should not be allowed to assign their UBIs.[6] Moreover, it is possible that seeing individuals in abject poverty and knowing they wasted the chance to receive a steady UBI might undercut political support for the project.

Elsewhere, one of us has offered a tentative compromise: allowing adults over the age of eighteen to assign benefits for a limited period (for example, twelve months) in exchange for a loan.[7] Limited assignability would still expand credit access for low-income individuals, while minimizing the risk that some older folks might be consigned to life-long poverty because of poor decisions in their youth.

Lastly, assignability raises a distinct but related question. Should the government be able to garnish (that is, seize) one's UBI for back taxes, child support, or other purposes?[8] Let's start with the impact on the debtor. Allowing garnishment would mean that a UBI might not lift the delinquent debtor out of poverty, as most or all of their UBI might be diverted. Such a result might be untenable to those who focus on outcomes. On the other hand, allowing garnishment for child support would increase the welfare of the parent/child units to whom the child support is owed, which is consistent with using a UBI to improve outcomes. A compromise for outcome-focused UBI supporters might be to allow garnishment for child support but not back taxes or most other purposes (which would harm only the debtor but not aid a third party). Those whose concern is equal opportunity would likely allow garnishment in all cases. Why should the government tolerate one's delinquency in supporting a child? And why should an individual who owes money to the government receive even more without having to repay their initial debt?[9]

21

HOW FREQUENTLY WOULD A BASIC INCOME BE PAID?

As we've mentioned, one defining feature of a UBI is that it is a series of regular payments. Just how frequent would these payments be? Most UBI proposals and pilot programs envision monthly payments, which mirrors the schedule for the most common existing benefit programs in the United States and many other countries. Elsewhere, one of us has advocated for even more frequent, bi-weekly payments, and policymakers could theoretically choose any payment schedule they like.[1]

Why would monthly (or bi-weekly) payments likely become the norm? In the abstract, payment frequency should be irrelevant. One can convert a once-in-a-lifetime or annual lump sum into a stream of more frequent payments by purchasing an annuity; as we just discussed, one can also theoretically borrow against a future stream of payments to acquire a lump sum today. In fact, lottery winners often convert a stream of future payments into one lump sum. If financial institutions began making such options accessible to most people, the payment schedule would be a minor detail.

But in today's world, payment frequency matters. Most importantly, a more frequent schedule helps the poorest households smooth their consumption. Such households generally have limited access to credit and savings vehicles, which—when combined with the stress of poverty—makes it difficult for them to spread out their spending over a long payment cycle. As a result, many households must make do with less food and other necessities near the end of more stretched-out payment cycles. When they do have access to credit, they are generally relegated to high-interest credit cards or payday loans. When benefit payments finally come, more must go to interest and fees, making it harder to break even the next time around, let alone save anything.

Economists have observed this phenomenon even with monthly payments, describing a "Food Stamp nutrition cycle," in which caloric intake declines by 10 to 15% over the course of each month.[2] Similar declines in doctor visits and test scores, and increases in school disciplinary incidents, have also been observed. As a result, a consensus is emerging in food policy circles that more frequent payments (such as bi-weekly or semi-monthly) would improve outcomes by allowing beneficiaries to more easily smooth their consumption.[3]

On the other hand, a less frequent schedule may have its own benefits. First, a longer window between payments can operate as a forced savings mechanism that helps beneficiaries save up for significant expenses, such as appliances and new cars. Low-income households—especially those with limited access to banks—often find it hard to save for larger expenditures. In fact, many recipients report intentionally over-withholding (having one's employer withhold more estimated taxes than necessary from each paycheck) throughout the year in order to receive a bigger refund each tax season. EITC beneficiaries also recount that the lump sum nature encourages recipients to mentally account for the EITC as a "windfall." For a few weeks after receiving their refund, this gives recipients mental permission to spend it on small treats like gifts, eating out, and vacations that they otherwise forego due to tight finances.[4]

Reflecting these reports, some past experience with the EITC suggests that at least a portion of the working poor prefers yearly lump sum payments to a more frequent schedule. For example, from 1979 to 2010, families could choose to receive some of their EITC payments in advance in monthly installments. Take up was rather low, however, never exceeding 2% of those families.[5]

It is unclear, however, whether that hesitancy reflects a true preference for lump sum distribution in general, or springs from factors specific to the EITC. First, many recipients were unaware of the ability to receive payments in advance. Second, others feared having to repay EITC payments that turned out to be overly generous, as the payments began before eligibility was officially confirmed on a tax return. This fear is not trivial, given the complexity of determining the amount of EITC for which one is eligible. Further, many participants in a more recent pilot in Chicago expressed satisfaction with the ability to get EITC payments quarterly throughout the year instead of waiting for one lump sum.[6] Finally, the rise of refund anticipation loans offered by paid preparers to EITC recipients suggests that at least some would like a different payment schedule.

In addition to public preferences, administrability also matters. Namely, transaction and monitoring costs increase with frequency. Workers paid via direct deposit bear a time cost when they check their bank accounts to make sure that their payments are deposited; those who are paid with paper checks must actually deposit them. The government also incurs costs each time it transfers money to individuals, although the costs associated with electronic transfers are negligible compared to those needed to mail paper checks.

Existing practices suggest that monthly, bi-weekly, or semi-monthly payments are all administratively feasible. The United States already makes SNAP, WIC, and TANF payments monthly. It recently experimented with offering the Child Tax Credit monthly, and has paid out the tax credits that help with health care premiums monthly for several years. Elsewhere, monthly or quarterly payments for child benefits and welfare programs are already the norm. Lastly, bi-weekly or semi-monthly payments predominate in the employment context, which seems to suggest that most people prefer relatively frequent payments. Otherwise, it is likely that employers would minimize transaction costs by reducing payment frequency.

22

WHICH AGENCY WOULD ADMINISTER THE BASIC INCOME?

So which agency would actually administer the UBI? In most countries, payment would likely be made by the taxing authority or social services agency via direct deposit to a bank account or debit card.[1] For example, the Revenue and Customs Department pays out the UK Child Benefit, while in Brazil, the Ministry of Social Development administers the *Bolsa Familia* program. In the United States, the most likely candidates would be either the Internal Revenue Service (IRS) or the Social Security Administration (SSA). Consider the SSA, which currently makes roughly $1 trillion per year in monthly payments to about 65 million beneficiaries.[2] While the system is not perfect, it is impressively accurate given the sheer numbers involved. In 2017, for example, only $1.2 million worth of payments to only 712 beneficiaries were misdirected.[3]

The IRS also has considerable experience transferring money directly to individuals. Most recently, it issued three sets of emergency relief payments—totaling $867 billion—during the first year-and-a-half of the Covid-19 pandemic.[4] And aside from the pandemic, it regularly pays refunds to individuals whose employers have over-withheld prepayments of taxes or who qualify for refundable tax credits such as the EITC or Child Tax Credit. In fiscal year 2020, for example, the IRS issued almost 122 million refunds totaling more than $736.2 billion.[5]

Although some commentators have suggested otherwise,[6] we believe that in the United States, the SSA is a more natural fit for administering a UBI for three reasons. The first is practical—it already makes *monthly* payments to almost a fifth of Americans.[7] In contrast, the IRS generally makes only annual payments (subject to a very limited number of exceptions). For this reason, it seems the SSA's infrastructure could be more easily scaled up for a monthly or bi-weekly UBI.

The other reasons are political. The American public has a much more favorable view of the SSA than the IRS.[8] One recent Pew Research Center survey shows that 66% of respondents view the SSA favorably versus 28% who view it unfavorably, while 55% view the IRS favorably and 40% view it unfavorably. Another fairly recent Pew survey even showed that in 2015, the share of respondents with unfavorable views of the IRS exceeded those with favorable views of the agency! A UBI is likely more politically palatable if its fate is not intertwined with the IRS.

The final point is related. Many Congresspeople regularly cast the IRS as a rogue agency that runs roughshod over the American public, hoping to starve it of cash.[9] Again, it seems more practical for the administration of a UBI to lie with an agency that is more secure in its funding and is somewhat more shielded from politics.

23

HOW WOULD A BASIC INCOME BE DELIVERED TO BENEFICIARIES?

Putting aside the "who" question, how would a UBI be delivered?[1] Direct deposit to a bank account is one likely option; current experience confirms this is viable on a fairly large scale. In the United States, more than 99% of Social Security beneficiaries use direct deposit,[2] and eight out of ten Americans receive their tax refunds this way.[3] Direct deposit is also used by roughly 85% of Alaskans to receive their permanent fund dividends.[4]

Direct deposit to a debit card is another option, and in fact, many cash-assistance programs in the United States have done this for the past two decades. Payments are deposited to an Electronic Benefits Transfer card, which recipients can use in stores, online, or to withdraw cash from cash machines. Similarly, the GiveDirectly pilot program in Africa deposits funds to mobile banking services accessed via cell phone; recipients can use the mobile money to purchase goods and services directly from merchants who accept it, or exchange it for cash from mobile money agents in the networks. In both structures, recipients need not have a bank account to receive benefits, which may be an advantage given the many lower-income individuals who lack access to financial institutions. Presumably, this would increase take-up by the very poorest, such as the homeless, who often find it difficult to access traditional benefits without a home address.

That said, direct deposit to bank accounts could induce the unbanked to set up accounts.[5] Consider Mongolia, which distributes revenue from minerals and mining into accounts set up for minors. By essentially requiring parents who want their children to receive benefits to open savings accounts in their names, Mongolia has the highest percentage of adults with a bank account—92%—in the developing world. Perhaps more impressively, 93% of Mongolians aged 15–24 also own accounts. Iran also saw large increases in account ownership after restricting delivery of household energy dividends to bank accounts.[6]

A final alternative—one about which we are more skeptical—is to use a cryptocurrency such as Ethereum or Bitcoin.[7] Hedge for Humanity[8] and Democracy.Earth,[9] two US-based nonprofits, are each already offering blockchain-based UBIs. Democracy.Earth claims that its UBI token (which it streams to Ethereum addresses) will "provide universal access to liquidity that serves to inhibit financial coercion of public decisions" and will "[establish] the bedrock for the infrastructure required to make a Universal Basic Income (UBI) mechanism that can reach everyone on earth." While the goals of accessibility, anti-coercion, and democratic, autonomous organizations are certainly consistent with a UBI, we are not yet convinced that using crypto or blockchain is superior to existing direct deposit systems to bank accounts, debit cards, or mobile devices. In fact, it seems to exclude less-sophisticated individuals, as crypto currently often requires a user to take a series of steps to convert it into a form that is usable in the real world. For example, to convert cryptocurrencies to dollars, users generally must sell them on a crypto exchange, although some cryptocurrencies can be converted to cash at special ATMs or used via special debit cards that draw from one's crypto account. The spread of such ATMs and debit cards may make crypto more attractive as an alternative in the future.

Part 3

COMMON ALTERNATIVES

24

HOW DOES A BASIC INCOME COMPARE TO TRADITIONAL WELFARE PROGRAMS?

A UBI differs from traditional welfare programs along multiple dimensions. Most importantly, a UBI provides a steady stream of cash that people can use however they like, no strings attached. In contrast, many traditional welfare programs provide in-kind transfers (free school lunches), vouchers for specific goods or services (food stamps), or cash with limits on where the aid can be spent. Chapter 25 addresses this distinction in more detail.

Second, a UBI is universal. Everyone gets it. You do not need to prove that your income or wealth is under a certain threshold. You don't have to be a parent or caregiver, unlike many welfare programs that favor parents and families. You receive it whether you are single or married, young or old, healthy or not, rural or urban. It does not pick and choose which groups of people deserve aid.

Third, a UBI is unconditional. As chapter 26 explores, you need not prove that you are working, looking for work, or unable to work for an "acceptable" reason such as disability, caring for a child or elderly relative, or participating in a job training program. You don't need to pass a drug test, prove that you have a spotless criminal record, or show that your child is going to school regularly.

Although these are the most important substantive distinctions, there are several practical differences as well. A UBI would be automatic, negating the need for complicated application forms and time-consuming office visits. It would provide a uniform amount that did not vary based on hours worked or one's wages. A UBI would be paid at frequent intervals, in contrast to once-a-year tax credits, and it would be paid throughout one's life, in contrast to child allowances or pensions for the elderly.

The following chapters explore these distinctions in more detail.

HOW DOES A BASIC INCOME COMPARE TO IN-KIND OR RESTRICTED CASH TRANSFERS?

One defining feature of a UBI is that unlike in-kind and restricted cash transfers, it comes with no strings attached. Recipients can use the payments however they think best—for rent, food, clothing, or a laptop for a child.

This freedom is most obvious when you compare a UBI to in-kind transfers, which provide a single or very small set of options. A child who receives lunch under the National School Lunch Program is limited to whatever the school offers; public housing tenants are limited to whatever apartments are available.

But even many cash or cash-like transfers still contain numerous restrictions. Take SNAP, which is the current version of what used to be called "food stamps" and which is the second largest federal anti-poverty program in the United States. Not only are beneficiaries limited to using SNAP benefits solely for food, but there are also rules about which foods can be purchased! For example, SNAP recipients cannot purchase "hot food" such as a ready-to-eat roasted chicken.

The Women, Infants and Children (WIC) nutritional program (funded federally but administered by states) is even more limiting. California has a 17-page pamphlet identifying which foods WIC beneficiaries can purchase—white eggs but not brown; blocks of cheese but not shredded or sliced cheese; salad mixes only if they do not contain "added ingredients" such as dressing, cheese, or croutons.[1] And for some items—such as yogurt, cereal, and pasta—only specific brands are eligible.

In some cases, even seemingly unrestricted cash welfare programs have limits. Take TANF, which is closest to what people typically think of as "welfare." TANF generally delivers aid through "electronic benefit transfer" or "EBT" cards that work like debit cards, and federal law requires states to take steps to prevent beneficiaries from using those cards at liquor stores, gambling establishments, and strip clubs.[2] Many states impose their own additional restrictions. Kansas, for example, prohibits using EBT cards at movie theaters, swimming pools, sporting events, jewelry stores, and nail salons, as well as to purchase tobacco, tattoos, and body piercings.[3]

In contrast, a UBI has no restrictions on its use. UBI supporters emphasize two benefits from this freedom. The first is moral—unrestricted cash transfers promote recipients' autonomy and self-ownership by allowing individuals to determine for themselves what would be best for them. In contrast, in-kind transfers are paternalistic and imply both a distrust of recipients and value judgments about what recipients "should" and "should not" spend money on. The second is pragmatic—a UBI is more efficient than traditional welfare programs, at both the provider and beneficiary levels.[4] We'll talk more about these arguments, and objections to them, in chapters 41 and 42.

HOW DOES A BASIC INCOME COMPARE TO PROGRAMS FOR THE UNEMPLOYED AND DISABLED?

The universal and unconditional nature of a UBI also sets it apart from benefits targeted to the unemployed and disabled. These programs attempt to distinguish the "deserving" from the "undeserving" on the theory that people who choose not to work do not merit aid, but those who wish to work but are unable to do so for reasons beyond their control do deserve help. By tying aid to the involuntary inability to work, however, such programs may inadvertently discourage people from working.

As chapter 50 explores, distinguishing between the voluntarily and involuntarily unemployed has a long history and feels intuitive to many. Aiding those who choose not to work strikes many as unfair, often due to concerns about reciprocity and incentives. UBI supporters generally respond to these arguments in two ways. Many advocates, especially left-leaning ones, reject them on a philosophical level. In their view, every citizen deserves aid—whether or not he or she could work in the paid labor market, and whether or not the state could accurately distinguish between who can and cannot work. Although some might concede that programs targeted to the unemployed and disabled serve some separate purpose, they do not serve the purposes of UBI and are therefore normatively insufficient.

Other advocates, primarily conservatives and libertarians, favor a UBI over programs targeted to the unemployed and disabled for pragmatic reasons.[1] If decision-makers could accurately assess who was and wasn't capable of work, and if such programs could be designed to minimize work disincentives, these UBI advocates might change their tune. But these supporters acknowledge that programs for the unemployed and disabled generally do an extremely poor job of identifying the work-capable for numerous reasons.

Many disabilities that render someone incapable of work, such as major depressive disorder and other mental illnesses, can be difficult to prove. Disagreement also exists as to what counts as a disability, with the definition changing over time. Currently, more than a third of disability beneficiaries in the United States and over 60% of nonelderly SSI beneficiaries are diagnosed with a mental disorder. Yet before the 1980s, people struggling with illnesses such as major depressive disorder had a difficult time qualifying for such benefits.[2] Alcoholism and drug addiction were not considered disabilities for many decades, were briefly recognized as such by the early 1990s, and then were demoted from such status in 1996. Moreover, federal courts and agencies are all over the map even when it comes to which professionals are qualified to assess whether or not a claimant is indeed disabled![3]

Not surprisingly, obtaining disability benefits is extremely cumbersome, and a cottage industry of books and paid professionals has sprung up to assist claimants. For all these reasons, often the very people who can convince decision-makers that they are disabled and cannot work are actually higher functioning and *more* capable of work than those who are less convincing. The high error rates found during audits of SSA disability determinations illustrate these difficulties. For example, studies suggest a rate of improper benefit denials (i.e., "false negatives") of anywhere from 20–60% of the total number of denials.[4] While providing an unconditional benefit may be over-inclusive, trying to weed out who is capable of work results in under-inclusivity. Reasonable people differ on which is the worse error.

Another pragmatic concern is that explicitly tying aid to the inability to work actually encourages people not to work. For example, in the United States, collecting disability benefits turns on being unable to engage in "substantial gainful activity," which is defined as earning more than a threshold amount; that sum was $1,350 per month in 2022. Individuals who earn even a dollar more than that amount will lose their SSI disability benefits, which can be up to

$841 per month for a single person.[5] Losing $841 in benefits due to a single extra dollar of earned income creates an effective marginal tax rate on that 1,351st dollar of 84,100%! Although nothing about disability benefits necessitates the use of such "cliff effects," many such programs contain them.

Intuition and anecdotal reports similarly suggest that programs that pay people not to work so long as they are "disabled" will encourage some to be less than diligent in attempting to recover from what might otherwise be a temporary disability, or in adapting to a permanent disability. (Of course, whether a disability is temporary or permanent, and the extent to which one can minimize the impact of a permanent disability, is beyond many people's control. But it's not unrealistic to imagine that some people have some agency in these situations.) Unemployment benefits likewise contain perverse incentives. To discourage individuals from voluntarily leaving jobs to collect benefits, they assist people who are laid off but not those who leave their jobs voluntarily. While this goal generally makes sense, it can also trap people in jobs when they can see the end is near. Such individuals are incentivized to stay until they are laid off—instead of leaving voluntarily and taking the time to find a job that is a better fit.

27

HOW DOES A BASIC INCOME COMPARE WITH BENEFITS FOR WORKERS, LIKE THE EARNED INCOME TAX CREDIT?

The unconditional nature of a UBI also sets it apart from a variety of tax and other benefits targeted to working families. These programs— such as the EITC in the United States, the Working Tax Credit (WTC) in the United Kingdom, and the Canada Workers Benefit (CWB) in Canada, are UBI-like in that they provide cash transfers to families that have no restrictions on how they can be spent. They differ from a UBI in several key ways, however. Most notably, they are available only to individuals who have paying jobs in the market economy.

To illustrate, consider the EITC. Depending on family size, it provides a tax credit equal to a percentage of a worker's income, up to a ceiling amount. The size of the credit remains level until earnings hit another threshold, at which point the credit gradually phases out with each additional dollar of income until it reaches zero. (The United States is not alone in using this structure; in-work benefits in Belgium, Canada, Finland, France, Germany, Hungary, New Zealand, and the United Kingdom also increase and then decrease with earned income.[1])

Economists generally agree that this structure encourages work for earners in the phase-in range, whose benefits increase with income. But they disagree about whether it discourages work for earners near the phase-out range, although it is the case that EITC benefits decrease less sharply with each dollar of earned income than under most traditional welfare programs.

Importantly, the EITC is refundable. If the amount of credit exceeds the individual's tax liability, the government transfers the difference to the individual. Like the EITC, most in-work credits outside the United States are refundable, although those in Belgium, Finland, Germany, the Netherlands, and Sweden are not.[2] This distinction is crucial when a tax credit is used to benefit low-income individuals, since many low-income individuals have little to no income tax liability.

Substantively, the EITC differs from a UBI in three key aspects. Most notably, the EITC and its cousins elsewhere are explicitly tied to work in the paid labor market. Individuals with no earned income—regardless of the reason—receive no benefit. To UBI supporters, this means that the neediest individuals receive no help; to UBI detractors, this incentivizes those who can work to do so. And as currently designed, the more one earns, the larger a credit one receives (up to the ceiling); the less one earns, the less one receives. As a result, the very poorest benefit less than the merely "somewhat poor." A UBI would most certainly not decrease when earned income *decreases*, regardless of whether a "true" UBI would decrease as income *increases* (see chapter 8). Moreover, the EITC and similar credits are counter-cyclical. They provide fewer benefits during economic downturns when one is working less or working at a reduced wage—exactly when citizens might need assistance the most.[3]

A second key substantive difference is that in many countries (including the United States, Canada, France, and Ireland) the size of the benefit depends in part on the number of children in a household.[4] The difference is starkest in the United States. For much of the EITC's existence, childless workers received almost no benefit. In 2020, for example, the maximum credit for a childless worker was $538, compared to $3,584 for individuals with one child; $5,920 for two children; and $6,660 for three or more children.[5] Although the difference is less pronounced elsewhere, Canada, France, Ireland, and New Zealand also provide benefits that depend to some extent on the number of children in a household.

Setting aside whether a UBI would be paid to children, a true UBI would not treat adults with the same income unequally in this manner. And as UBI proponents note, these family status provisions have negative practical consequences. First, simply understanding the various family arrangement rules is difficult and often creates unintended errors. Second, the family status provisions may encourage unmarried parents either to arrange custody so as to maximize tax benefits or to fudge which children live with which parent. In contrast, the simplicity of a UBI alleviates some of these distortions. Although a UBI would still need rules to determine which parent would receive a child's UBI, the fact that family size would not otherwise shape the size of an adult's UBI lowers the stakes of these rules.

The third key substantive difference is that the EITC (along with similar benefits in Canada, the United Kingdom, Ireland, France, and New Zealand) is determined on a household basis, whereas UBI proponents envision a UBI as an individual entitlement.[6] This, coupled with phase-ins and phase-outs, creates marriage penalties in several countries. In the United States, two single parents with two children each would see their total EITC benefits reduced by over one-third if they married! In contrast, a key feature of a UBI is that it would not vary by marital status.

Additionally, in-work tax credits differ from a UBI administratively. As discussed more in chapter 21, tax credits are generally paid annually, whereas a UBI would likely be paid monthly or bi-weekly. A second difference is that tax credits are by definition part of the tax system, and can only be claimed by individuals who file a tax return. Moreover, they are often exceedingly complex—the IRS booklet explaining the EITC, for example, clocks in at forty-one pages long![7] This spurs many low-income households to use paid preparers for assistance, creating an incongruous Catch-22 in which beneficiaries have to spend money to obtain a cash antipoverty benefit. Moreover, this complexity contributes to improper payments, which can in turn contribute to high audit rates.[8] Presumably, a UBI's simplicity would counter these problems.

In other ways, however, an in-work credit and a UBI share positive attributes when compared to traditional welfare programs. Situating such credits within the tax system reduces stigma and increases take-up when compared to other welfare programs. A UBI would likely have even more take up, with the same (or less) stigma than the EITC and its cousins. Finally, they tend to be fairly administratively efficient. The EITC, for example, has much lower overhead costs than traditional anti-poverty programs, roughly 1% of benefits paid out;[9] one would expect a UBI to have similar costs.

28

HOW DOES A BASIC INCOME COMPARE WITH CHILD ALLOWANCES OR CHILD TAX CREDITS?

The UBI also overlaps in some respects with the child-specific cash allowances offered by numerous countries. But as with many social benefit programs, the details vary from country to country. The United Kingdom, Ireland, Canada, and most European countries provide what is most commonly referred to as a "Child Benefit" or a "Child Allowance," which generally provide a few hundred dollars per month.[1] A family with two children, for example, would receive $246.25 per month in Sweden, $478.66 in Germany, and $556.90 per month in Luxembourg. Like a UBI, these allowances generally do not require recipient families to work to receive benefits. When it comes to other hallmarks of universality, however, child allowance benefits vary more widely. For example, countries such as the United Kingdom, Canada, France, and Germany means-test their allowances in some way, while countries such as Ireland provide a universal amount to all, regardless of income. In most countries, families receive the same amount per child regardless of family size, while in France the per-child amount differs slightly based on the number of children.

The United States does not provide a universal child allowance per se, but instead offers a partially refundable tax credit for families with children. As currently structured, the CTC provides larger benefits to families with earned income, while still providing some benefits to parents who are not employed in the formal labor market. In this sense, it differs from a true UBI and from the allowances and credits elsewhere, which generally provide benefits to parents regardless of work status. In addition to phasing in with work, the CTC also phases out for middle-income taxpayers and disappears completely for upper-income taxpayers. However, the size of each child's credit neither varies based on family size nor the child's age. Unlike most other countries' child allowances, the CTC has traditionally been paid annually, although the United States experimented with monthly advance payments in 2021.

These benefits all differ from a UBI in the fundamental sense that they are paid only to families with children, while a UBI is paid either to all adults or to all individuals regardless of age. Setting that distinction aside, they share one key feature of a UBI: they provide cash to families, and that cash allows parents to determine how best to provide for their children. In a sense, these child allowances can be thought of as "UBIs for children."

Not surprisingly, families receiving these benefits increase spending in ways that benefit children. Survey data from the US Census shows that over 90% of low-income families spent their enhanced 2021 child tax credit on basic needs (think food, utilities, rent, and transportation) as well as child-specific items (education, children's clothing, and child care). Recent work on the Canada Child Benefit similarly found that low-income families used additional funds not only for necessities like food and transportation but also childcare and education-related expenditures.[2]

Numerous analyses of families receiving these and similar cash and cash-like government benefits have found associations between larger family income and a variety of measures of children's well-being. Studies of the EITC and the Canada Child Benefit have found associations with higher math and reading scores;[3] other studies have found an association with increased high school and college graduation rates.[4] Not surprisingly, children from such families are also more likely to be employed in young adulthood, and studies have also found that adults whose families had received the EITC as children had higher incomes as adults.[5] At least one study of children from families receiving food stamps, a near-cash benefit, found a similar decrease in later rates of incarceration.[6] Other research shows an association between the EITC and measures of maternal and infant health such as increases in birth-weight and decreases in preterm birth.[7]

These results mirror those from studies on the impact of nongovernmental cash transfer programs on children. Consider the Eastern Cherokee casino payments (discussed in chapter 4). One study found that children in households receiving casino payments had higher levels of educational attainment than those not receiving them; the $4,000 annual transfer to each household correlated with one additional year of schooling for each child. The same study also found a lower incidence of criminal behavior among children in households receiving transfers, with no effect on parents' labor force participation.[8]

These studies confirm what might seem obvious to many readers: giving cash to families makes them measurably better off.[9] Columbia University researchers have recently quantified these benefits; they argue that each $1 spent on the Child Tax Credit brings over $8 in returns to society, based on the indicators above.

One final point. Despite the fact that money is fungible, evidence suggests that the way benefits are framed matters given that people frequently engage in mental accounting. For example, recipients of the enhanced 2021 child tax credit payments reported more expenditures specifically related to children than after the earlier, general Covid-relief stimulus payments.[10] This mirrors what happened after the United Kingdom reformed its child allowance scheme in the 1970s. Before the reform, the allowance consisted of two payments, one of which was a tax allowance that was typically reflected as higher take-home pay to the father of the family. The reform consolidated the subsidies as a single nontaxable payment directly to the mother, and spending on children's clothing, children's shoes, toys, and children's pocket money increased.[11]

Providing cash benefits to families with children—and especially benefits earmarked specifically for children—has long-run positive impacts. Moreover, it is quite popular. People generally don't have the same objections to providing benefits to children as they do to providing benefits to adults. As we have discussed in chapter 14, this suggests that a well-designed UBI would include children. At the very least, any UBI that excluded children should be coupled with an unconditional child benefit.

29

HOW DOES A BASIC INCOME COMPARE TO A NEGATIVE INCOME TAX?

We've now seen the similarities and differences between a UBI and a variety of existing benefit programs. How does a UBI compare to other common proposals for *new* redistributive programs? For example, you might have heard about the concept of a Negative Income Tax (NIT), which Milton Friedman popularized as a means of replacing existing welfare programs.[1] An NIT sounds very different from a UBI because, well, it sounds like a tax, not a benefit! But as we'll see, in most circumstances, the two are mathematically equivalent. Friedman's coauthor (and spouse) Rose Friedman described the idea as follows:

> The basic idea of a negative income tax is simple . . . Under the current positive income tax you are permitted to receive a certain amount of income without paying any tax . . . This amount is composed of a number of elements—personal exemptions . . . standard deduction . . . [etc.] To simplify the discussion, let us use the simpler British term of "personal allowances" to refer to this basic amount.
>
> If your income exceeds your allowances, you pay a tax on the excess at rates that are graduated according to the size of the excess. Suppose your income is less than the allowances? Under the current system, those unused allowances in general are of no value. You simply pay no tax . . .
>
> With a negative income tax, you would receive from the government some fraction of the unused allowances . . . When your

income was above allowances, you would pay tax, the amount depending on the tax rates charged on various amounts of income. When your income was below allowances, you would receive a subsidy, the amount depending on the subsidy rates attributed to various amounts of unused allowances.[2]

To illustrate, imagine a negative income tax with a personal allowance of $30,000 and a tax rate of 20% on all income above $30,000.[3] Individuals with incomes below $30,000 will receive a payment that equals 20% of the difference between $30,000 and their pre-tax income. Thus:

- *Amy*, who earns $0, receives a net transfer from the government equal to 20% of her unused $30,000 allowance, or $6,000 (20% × (0 – $30,000) = –$6,000; i.e., a subsidy of $6,000);
- *Bruno*, who earns $30,000, owes nothing and is owed nothing; and
- *Chloe*, who earns $60,000, pays a tax of 20% on all her income above $30,000, or $6,000 (20% × ($60,000 – $30,000) = $6,000).

This is mathematically equivalent to a UBI coupled with a tax on non-UBI income. Imagine a UBI of $6,000 paid to all regardless of income coupled with a 20% tax on all other income, with no exemption amount. Thus:

- *Amy*, who earns $0, receives a UBI payment of $6,000 but pays no tax, resulting in a net transfer from the government to *Amy* of $6,000;
- *Bruno*, who earns $30,000, receives a UBI payment of $6,000 but pays tax of $6,000 (20% of $30,000), resulting in a net transfer of zero;
- *Chloe*, who earns $60,000, receives a UBI payment of $6,000 but pays tax of $12,000 (20% of $60,000), resulting in a net transfer from *Chloe* to the government of $6,000.

And both are mathematically equivalent to a UBI that explicitly phases out with income. Consider a UBI of $6,000 that phases out at a 20% rate starting with one's first dollar of non-UBI income that is coupled with a 20% tax on non-UBI income over $30,000. Such a UBI fully phases out once income hits $30,000 (20% × $30,000 = $6,000). Thus:

- *Amy*, who earns $0, receives a UBI of $6,000 and pays no income tax, for a net transfer from the government of $6,000;
- *Bruno*, who earns $30,000, receives no UBI (his UBI fully phases out) and pays no income tax, for a net transfer of zero; and
- *Chloe*, who earns $60,000, receives no UBI (again, on account of the phaseout) and pays income tax of $6,000 (20% × ($60,000 – $30,000)), for a net transfer to the government of $6,000.

The first example involves an NIT; the second involves a UBI that doesn't explicitly phase out coupled with a tax on all non-UBI income; and the third involves a UBI that explicitly phases out with income and is coupled with a tax on non-UBI income over an exemption amount. But all result in the same net transfers between *Amy, Bruno, Chloe,* and the government.

Three points about these examples. First, although they use a flat rate of 20%, the equivalence holds in tax systems that use graduated rate structures. Second, they envision individuals as the taxable unit, while the tax systems of the United States and a few European countries (such as France and Germany) generally use families. Nothing mandates, however, that an income tax system use the family instead of an individual as the taxable unit, and in fact, many OECD countries use the individual.

Third, the examples assume that an income tax will fund a UBI. The *sole* circumstance in which an NIT and UBI are not economically equivalent is if a UBI is funded solely from sources other than taxes on income (or a base strongly correlated with income). Imagine a UBI funded solely by revenue from auctioning off the broadband spectrum. In such a case, *Amy, Bruno,* and *Chloe* each receive $6,000, regardless of their income, since the revenue from firms that purchase broadband spectrum is not correlated with their individual incomes. But as we discuss in chapter 12, almost every serious UBI proposal of any significant scope would require some, if not all, of its funding from increased taxes on income or a base like consumption that strongly correlates to income.

Assuming that a UBI will be at least partially funded by income taxes, we can see that the key difference between a UBI and an NIT is one of optics.[4] A UBI appears to be just that—universal—while an NIT is explicitly tied to one's income. UBI proponents argue that universal framing is key to minimizing the stigma associated with poverty, and that a drawback of an NIT is that it—like traditional welfare programs—explicitly targets the poor. And it may be the case that such framing increases support among some members of the public, given the popularity of seemingly universal programs like Social Security and Medicare. But it may also reduce support in other quarters. NIT proponents argue that the superficial universality of a UBI undermines its political viability, due to the "Why are we paying a UBI to Jeff Bezos?" rejoinder.

30

HOW DOES A BASIC INCOME COMPARE WITH PROPOSALS LIKE BABY BONDS OR A BASIC ENDOWMENT?

Another program you may hear about is a "basic endowment," "stakeholder grant," or "baby bond," variations of which have been recently proposed by Senator and former 2020 presidential candidate Cory Booker as well as economist Thomas Piketty. Let's start with a basic endowment or stakeholder grant (also called a "stake"). Like a UBI, these are no-strings-attached cash transfers to all citizens. But unlike a UBI, a basic endowment or stake is a lump sum transfer paid in one or a few installments. The concept traces its roots back to Thomas Paine, who in 1796 proposed the creation of a "national fund, out of which there shall be paid to every person, when arrived at the age of twenty-one years, the sum of fifteen pounds sterling, as a compensation in part, for the loss of his or her natural inheritance, by the introduction of the system of landed property."[1]

More recently, legal scholars Bruce Ackerman and Anne Alstott popularized the concept in their 1999 book *The Stakeholder Society*.[2] They proposed providing each citizen a stake of $80,000[3] that could be used for any reason—to pay for college, start a business, buy a home, or save for the future. The stake would be paid in four annual installments, with the first generally occurring at age 21, but those enrolling in post-secondary education would receive their stakes earlier. Ackerman and Alstott proposed funding their plan with a 2% tax on net wealth, plus requiring "repayment" at death (with interest) from those with estates over $50,000.

Several European countries have experimented with much smaller yet similar programs colloquially referred to as "baby bonuses." For example, from 2005 to 2011, the United Kingdom's "Child Trust Fund" paid £250 for each newborn child; those in the poorest third of households received an additional £250.[4] From 2007 to 2010, Spain paid a "universal birth bonus" of 2,500 Euros per child; in Belgium the parents of newborns receive a "birth premium" (prime de naissance) of roughly 1,160 Euros per child.[5]

And in the United States, Senator Booker has proposed a somewhat similar program, colloquially referred to as a "baby bond," which would deposit $1,000 into a savings account for each new baby at birth.[6] Each following year until age 18, up to $2,000 (depending upon family income) would be added to the account. No withdrawals would be allowed until age 18, at which time beneficiaries could begin withdrawing funds for specified purposes such as education and purchasing a home.

As discussed in chapter 21, the recipient of a lump sum transfer can convert it into a stream of more frequent payments by buying an annuity; in theory, the opposite is also true.[7] If this could be done easily, then the difference between a basic endowment and a basic income would be largely cosmetic, but for the longevity concerns discussed below. Yet most basic income proposals prohibit recipients from transferring away their right to future payments for one larger lump sum immediately, reflecting a normative preference for regular lifetime payments. Why?

One concern is the risk that one might waste his or her endowment grant. Most basic endowment proponents explicitly ground their proposals in equality of opportunity concerns (in contrast to equality of outcomes). Ackerman and Alstot write that a stake would "give each citizen an equal opportunity to . . . shap[e] her life. By the time Americans reach early adulthood, they have encountered vastly unequal chances to define themselves, realize their talents, and move with financial confidence into the workplace."[8] A stake helps put young adults on a more even economic playing field. Each citizen can "taste the joys and sorrows of real freedom—and the possibilities of learning from his own successes and mistakes."[9] On this view, the risk someone might waste a grant is part and parcel of the normative justification for the endowment itself.

Many UBI proponents, in contrast, have other concerns. According to Philippe Van Parijs, for example, a "basic income is about providing economic security throughout life."[10] To these advocates, the consequences of a young adult blowing his or her stake must be taken seriously. In their view, the types of people who would succeed regardless of the financial status of their youth are the very same people who are more likely to make good use of a lump sum received in early adulthood. Those who already have the chips stacked against them (perhaps they are simply less intelligent, less industrious, or less well-connected) are more likely to waste their stakes.[11] To Van Parijs and friends, a basic income has all the upsides of a basic endowment without the downsides—it both protects us from youthful mistakes and gives us the freedom to make investments and take risks throughout our lives.[12]

Ackerman and Alstott offer two responses. Broadly, they argue that beneficiaries are more likely to waste a basic income that they receive in "dribs and drabs" than a large chunk of money that they receive all at once. They assume that the sheer size of the stake will lead to finance classes, reasoned discussions with parents, and thoughtful decisions about how best to use one's stake. More narrowly, they build two safeguards into their proposal. First, they limit full access to one's stake to high school graduates; dropouts are limited to the interest on their stake—in effect, a basic income. Second, they explicitly retain a pension for the elderly as protection against youthful mistakes.

A second normative difference between a basic endowment and a basic income concerns the nature of identity. Do people change so much throughout their lives that *Athena* at the age of 20 is not the same person as *Athena* at the age of 60? If so, then a basic endowment privileges the decisions 20-year-old *Athena* makes—sometimes to the detriment of 60-year-old *Athena*—whereas a UBI treats all our discontinuous selves equally. Or are 20-year-old and 60-year-old *Athena* the same person? Ackerman and Alstott believe so, asserting that even if the elder *Athena* has radically different life interests, she will view her 60-year-old self as inextricably connected to her 20-year-old self. They argue that "each of us has only one life, despite the fact that our experiences, desires, and ideals change over time. This life begins at birth and ends at death." To assert otherwise, they argue, treats us like eternal children.

The final normative difference relates to longevity.[13] A short-lived person is better off receiving a stake at the start of adulthood, whereas a long-lived person is better off receiving a basic income throughout her life. Which is preferable may well turn on the justification for the benefit. Take *Caroline*, who has a longer life expectancy than *Barnaby*. If the goal is providing a safety net throughout one's life, then a basic income ensures that both *Barnaby* and *Caroline* have an equally protective safety net over the course of their lives. In contrast, a lump sum would provide safety nets of unequal size, since *Caroline* would have less per year than *Barnaby* if they each converted their stake to an annuity. But if the goal is providing an equal start at adulthood, then an endowment ensures that both individuals have equal seed money. In contrast, a UBI would not generate equal seed money, since presumably *Barnaby* would not be able to convert his UBI to as large a lump sum as *Caroline* based on actuarial values.

31

HOW DOES A BASIC INCOME DIFFER FROM A GUARANTEED EMPLOYMENT PROGRAM?

A final frequently mentioned alternative to a UBI is a guaranteed employment program. By now, you can probably guess how the two differ! As we've seen, a UBI is an unconditional transfer program. This means that individuals are eligible to receive the benefit whether they are working or not, or even whether they are trying to work or not. Many people see this as a significant problem with the UBI (see chapter 6, chapters 49–50). At the very least, such people would prefer a transfer program which did not (in their eyes) discourage work. But maybe an even better idea would be a transfer program that actually *required* work.

The United States already has some transfer programs that require work as a condition of eligibility, such as the EITC (see chapter 26). But the EITC doesn't do anything for people who would *like* to work, but are unable to find a job on their own. It therefore still leaves a significant portion of the poor unprovided for.

A more radical solution would thus be a guaranteed employment program, or "job guarantee." On this approach, the government would create a number of jobs in areas that are underserved by the private sector, perhaps including infrastructure maintenance, child and elder care, and education, and make these jobs available to anyone unable to find work in the regular labor market. Rather than traditional welfare benefits, the government would give recipients a paycheck for work performed—presumably at a level high enough to support meaningful relief from poverty but low enough not to crowd out or disincentivize private sector work.[1]

There are several purported advantages of a job guarantee over a UBI. First, the net cost of a jobs program would likely be lower. This is both because benefits would be going to a smaller number of people (only those participating in the program instead of everyone), and because those receiving benefits would also be performing productive work, thereby offsetting the social cost of their pay. The second advantage is that a job guarantee ties benefits to *work*, and work is believed by many to have various psychological, sociological, and health benefits over idleness. Money is good for the poor; but money tied to work, it is claimed, is even better.[2]

Not everyone agrees, however, that a job guarantee would be superior to the simple, no-strings-attached cash grant of a UBI. For starters, such a program involves a great deal of faith in government to determine what kind of work is socially valuable, and to direct and manage that work in a reasonably efficient way. In the absence of the profit and loss signals that discipline firms in the private sector, and with the tendency of government programs to be captured and manipulated by powerful special interest groups, there is some reason to doubt that this faith is warranted. As labor leader Andy Stern argues, "a guaranteed jobs program would require a huge government bureaucracy . . . It'd be a lot easier and more efficient just to give people cash."[3]

There is also some danger that a job guarantee program will fail to deliver on the psychological benefits associated with regular employment. People take satisfaction in their work when they feel like they're doing something *meaningful*, and when they feel that their income is a just reward for their skill and effort. But if the jobs created by the government come to be seen as just "busywork," or if the income comes to be as simply another form of government handout, then this satisfaction might fail to materialize.[4]

Finally, some argue that a job guarantee perpetuates the questionable idea that everyone should be "working" in the sense of participating in the paid labor market. This idea is certainly widely held. But is it true? Is it healthy? Is it even sustainable in an age of increasing technological automation? Perhaps it's OK if some people do not "work," in this sense, but instead spend their time caring for children or elderly parents, volunteering, or engaging in other worthwhile activities. A UBI gives people this choice in a way that a job guarantee does not.

Of course, we don't necessarily have to choose between a UBI and a job guarantee. It is true that both have the potential to be very costly programs. But there is no reason why an appropriately modest version of both could not co-exist, in just the same way that a UBI could co-exist with various in-kind or means-tested social welfare programs.

Part 4

EXAMPLES

32

DOESN'T ALASKA HAVE SOMETHING LIKE A BASIC INCOME?

Part 2 described what a large-scale UBI might look like, some details of which are drawn from lessons learned from the programs discussed in part 3. But we've also learned a lot about how a larger UBI might work from some smaller UBI-like programs and experiments.

One of the most famous is the "Alaska Permanent Fund Dividend," which has issued annual cash payments to every Alaskan resident since 1982. Anyone who has lived in the state for one full calendar year is eligible for the payment, regardless of their age, wealth, employment, or family status. The Alaska Dividend is thus a genuine example of a universal basic income. Indeed, it is one of only *two* examples of a long-term, state-funded UBI at the time of this writing—the other is Iran's subsidy reform plan (see chapter 4).

The revenues for the Alaska Dividend come from the wealth generated by Alaskan oil. In 1976, the state began investing a small portion of that wealth in the newly created Alaska Permanent Fund. The idea was to ensure that wealth generated by the oil would benefit not only the current generation of Alaskans, but future generations as well.

Payments from the Alaska Dividend are based on the average financial return of the Fund over the previous five years. Typically, distributions are around $1,600 per person per year, but they have ranged from a low of $331 in 1984 to a high of $2,072 in 2015. And what makes the Dividend genuinely universal—unlike the majority of larger UBI proposals—is that these payments truly do not vary with income. The payments themselves are uniform. And because the funding is based on oil revenue—instead of a tax on income or something else that varies with income—no implicit means test is smuggled in the back door (see chapter 8 for more on this point).

Since its inception, the state has distributed over $22 billion in assistance under the program. This money seems to have made a real difference for Alaskans. One 2016 study found that the dividend lifts between 15,000 and 25,000 people out of poverty each year and reduces the number of Alaskans living in poverty by up to 20%.[1] It has reduced the incidence of low-birth-weight babies.[2] And it has proved extremely popular. According to one survey, 79% of Alaskans believe that the dividend is an important source of income for their community, and 85% believe that many people spend a large portion of the dividend in fulfilling basic needs.[3]

To what extent can the Alaska Dividend serve as a model for UBIs elsewhere? It is true that Alaska is unusual in the richness of its oil reserves. However, there is no reason why similar kinds of programs couldn't be developed elsewhere on the basis of *other* natural resources. States without oil could create funds based on the value of natural gas, mineral deposits, or even the land itself.

Taxing and redistributing the value of unimproved natural resources is an idea with a long and diverse pedigree. Since they are a free gift of nature, and not the creation of human labor, many people believe that natural resources ought to belong to (or at least work to the benefit of) everybody. So, a resource tax reflects many people's idea of fairness. At the same time, such a tax is also arguably more economically efficient than a tax on labor. Taxing labor leads to people working less, which isn't necessarily good. But taxing the raw value of resources doesn't reduce the availability of resources. It simply redistributes their value.

It should be no surprise, then, that the Alaska Fund has enjoyed wide and bipartisan support. On the one hand, it accords with ideas like that of the 20th-century progressive social reformer Henry George, who advocated a "Single Tax" as a recipe for ending exploitation, poverty, and crime. And on the other hand, it fits squarely with more conservative ideas about limited government and individual responsibility. As Alaskan Governor Jay Hammond put the point, "Alaska's dividend program is, of course, anything but socialistic. Socialism is government taking from a wealthy few to provide what government thinks is best for all. Permanent Fund Dividends do just the opposite. They take from the money which, by constitutional mandate, belongs to all and allows each individual to determine how to spend some of his or her share. What could be more capitalistic?"[4]

33

DIDN'T THE UNITED STATES RUN SOME EXPERIMENTS ON THE BASIC INCOME BACK IN THE 1970S?

You might have also heard about some older UBI experiments in the United States. Believe it or not, the United States came pretty close to passing a UBI into law in the late 1960s. And under the presidency of Richard Nixon, no less!

At the time, there was a great deal of interest in the idea of a UBI. Milton Friedman had popularized the idea of a Negative Income Tax in his 1962 book, *Capitalism and Freedom*.[1] (See chapter 29 for more on an NIT.) And in 1968, a letter authored by Friedman, Paul Samuelson, and several others received over 1,000 signatures from other economists and front-page coverage in the *New York Times*.[2] In 1969, the Nixon administration proposed a "Family Assistance Plan" that would pay up to $1,600 (around $13,000 in today's dollars) to a family of four, with payments declining as earnings rose. For a while, it looked like the proposal might be a bipartisan success. See chapter 64 for more on the Family Assistance Plan.

Against this backdrop, the Institute for Research on Poverty, with financing from the government's Office of Economic Opportunity, began a series of experiments to measure the effects of an NIT. The studies ran from 1968 to 1982 and would eventually develop into what the social scientist Gilbert Steiner would describe as "the most ambitious socioeconomic experiment ever undertaken in America without a base in legislation or executive order."[3] Thousands of families in New Jersey, Pennsylvania, Iowa, North Carolina, Seattle,

Denver, and Gary, Indiana, would receive payments, with total expenditures on the study exceeding $620 million in today's dollars. The amount of the payments varied, from 50% of the poverty line to 148%. So too did the phase-out rate (the rate at which payments would be reduced as recipients' income rose), from 30% to 75%. The payments were limited in time, from a low of two years in Iowa and North Carolina, to a maximum of nine years in Seattle/Denver.

The findings were mixed but were generally regarded as disappointing to advocates of a UBI. First, recipients appeared to work less, and the more they received, the less they worked. In the Seattle and Denver experiments, husbands who received payments were found to work 6–11% fewer hours per year, and wives to work 23–32% fewer hours.[4]

However, there are several reasons for discounting this finding. First, as Gary Burtless of the Brookings Institution noted in his writeup of the results, the experimenters relied on self-reported earnings information.[5] This is a major problem, since participants had a strong incentive to under-report their earnings in order to increase the size of the benefit for which they were eligible. Once the self-reports were cross-referenced with actual earnings data, the labor effects in the Gary experiment disappeared entirely, and those in the Seattle/Denver experiments shrunk dramatically.

Second, even if the decline in working hours was exactly as originally reported, it's not obvious that this is a bad thing. A 10% reduction in hours worked among husbands does not mean that men are dropping out of the labor market altogether and watching television all day. It could mean that some overworked parents simply work a bit less, allowing them to spend more time with their families. As one researcher commented, "Some of [the work response from these experiments] came from cutting down hours, say from 65 to 60 hours a week, which doesn't seem like a tragedy."[6] It could also mean that they are remaining unemployed longer between jobs, perhaps looking for a better match. Among the young, a reduction in hours worked seems often to have meant an increase in years spent in school. And among wives, a more significant reduction of hours worked often meant spending more time with children. There are costs to all of these outcomes, but none of them is unequivocally bad.

Even if we put aside the question of work disincentives, however, the results of the NIT experiments still pose a challenge for advocates of a UBI. The challenge is one of costs and benefits. The least generous program, which provided support at a level equal to 50% of the poverty rate, would have saved $4 billion in 1980 dollars compared to the then-existing welfare system. However, it would have left 92% of welfare families financially worse off. A more generous program, providing support equal to the poverty level, would have cost $30 billion *more* than traditional welfare, and still would have left 25% of families worse off.[7] Once again, we see the difficulty in designing a system that simultaneously achieves the twin goals of providing adequate support to the poor, while still keeping costs at a manageable level.

34

WHAT ABOUT CANADA?

Around the same time that the United States was running the NIT experiments just discussed, Canada was also experimenting with a UBI. This project—the Manitoba Basic Annual Income Experiment, or "MINCOME"—took place in the city of Dauphin from 1974 to 1979. The idea was that MINCOME would serve a temporary pilot for a universal and permanent program. That permanent program was never adopted, but as we will see (and unlike the experiments in the United States), this had nothing to do with the perceived results of the experiment.

One unique feature of MINCOME is that Dauphin was selected to serve as a "saturation site," meaning that *all* of the 10,000 residents of the city were eligible to receive payments, assuming their incomes were low enough to qualify. This not only gave researchers access to a broader base of data, but also allowed for the possibility of observing community-level effects: effects that arise only when a sufficiently large percentage of community members receive the benefit (see chapters 37 and 45).

Under the terms of the experiment, a family that earned no other income would receive a payment equal to 60% of Canada's threshold for "low-income." Every dollar earned from other sources would reduce this benefit by 50 cents.

Unfortunately, the experiment quickly ran into financial difficulties. Inflation combined with higher-than-expected unemployment meant that costs began to spiral out of control. In the glum economic context of the 1970s, political interest in the experiment waned, and while data was collected for four years, most of that data was put straight into an archive, unanalyzed.

It was not until around 2008—nearly thirty years after the experiment had ended—that the results of the experiment were uncovered and analyzed by economist Evelyn Forget. The results were striking, and overwhelmingly positive.[1] It is true that hours worked in the labor market declined somewhat, though the results were smaller than those found in the US experiments—between 1 and 5%. But this downside—if indeed it is a downside at all—seemed to be greatly outweighed by the benefits produced by cash payments. Hospitalizations declined by 8.5%—primarily due to a reduction in alcohol-related incidents and mental health issues. More adolescents finished high school rather than dropping out early to work. And people reported being able to do things that they simply hadn't been able to afford to do before—like send their children to the dentist.

Forget wrote up her analysis of the MINCOME experiment under the title, "The Town With No Poverty." And that analysis reignited interest in a UBI in Canada, which launched another pilot program in 2017—the Ontario Basic Income Project. Although intended to last for three years, the Ontario program wound up running for only a few months before being canceled by the newly elected Conservative government. Even so, a survey conducted by researchers at McMaster University suggested that the pilot was having positive effects on mental health and employment.[2]

Both the MINCOME experiment, then, and the later Ontario project demonstrate the fragility of support for UBI in shifting political climates. Building a lasting and stable coalition in support of a UBI, as we will discuss in part 7, will be a formidable challenge.

35

HAS A BASIC INCOME
EVER BEEN TRIED IN THE
DEVELOPING WORLD?

After the NIT and MINCOME experiments in the 1970s, interest in UBI waned for a bit before picking up again in the early 2000s. As we will see in the next chapter, there has been a large number of UBI experiments in North America and Europe over the last decade. But you might be surprised to learn that the very *first* UBI experiments of the 21st century took place in the developing world—and that one of the most exciting current experiments is going on there right now.

These experiments took place in Namibia (2008–2009), India (2011–2013), and Kenya (2016–present). They differ from earlier experiments in the United States and Canada in three important ways. First, experiments in the developing world have tested a UBI, rather than an NIT. This change partly reflects the different socio-economic contexts in which the experiments have taken place, and partly reflects changes in interest in the two sorts of policies during the intervening thirty years.

Second, experiments in the developing world have primarily been funded by private institutions, rather than governments. Unlike experiments in the United States and Canada, which were conceived as pilot programs for new domestic social welfare policies, these experiments were intended as a kind of private philanthropic aid, generally funded by organizations outside the target country itself.

Finally, these experiments took place in a context of dire poverty. This last difference is crucial because it meant that experimenters could avoid a serious problem affecting most other studies. As we have seen, one of the biggest challenges of a UBI is to provide a level of benefits that is high enough to make a real difference in people's lives, while at the same time keeping costs at a manageable level. In the developing world, however, even a relatively low level of benefits can have a tremendous impact. The Kenya experiment, for instance, provides recipients with just 75 cents per day. This helps to make even a long-term, widespread program relatively affordable.

The results of these experiments have been generally quite positive. In Namibia, researchers found significant decreases in poverty and child malnutrition. Alcohol consumption among recipients did not increase, as some had feared that it would. And people actually worked *more*, rather than less.[1]

In India, the UBI was found to positively impact health, to reduce the frequency of child labor, to decrease levels of household debt, to increase school attendance and performance, and to broaden women's occupational activities. Once again, recipients were found to work more than people in the control group, and alcohol consumption did not increase.[2]

The experiment in Kenya is still ongoing. Indeed, with a twelve-year timeline and 20,000 recipients, it promises to be the longest-running and largest UBI experiment ever. This is a significant advantage, since some results of a UBI might not show up during the one- or two-year timeframe that is more commonly used (see chapter 37 for discussion). The experiment is targeting 295 rural villages in the Western and Rift Valley regions of Kenya: forty-four of those villages (roughly 5,000 people) will receive a UBI over the full twelve years, while eighty villages (about 7,300 people) will receive the UBI for two years, and seventy-one villages (8,500 people) will receive two years' worth of UBI in one lump-sum payment (like an endowment grant, which we discuss in chapter 30).

Researchers hope to learn how the UBI affects economic, physical, and social well-being, as well as to discern any larger scale macroeconomic effects such as price changes and changes in the availability of different goods and services. So far, the results have been encouraging. During Covid-19, transfers were found to improve well-being on measures such as hunger, sickness, and depression.[3] Further results should be available soon on the website of the organization running the experiment, GiveDirectly.org.[4]

36

WHAT ARE SOME OTHER CURRENT BASIC INCOME EXPERIMENTS?

The programs and experiments we've just detailed are only the tip of the iceberg. Today, there are more ongoing UBI experiments than ever before. Indeed, in just the United States alone, there are currently more than forty pilot programs taking place in various cities across the country. This chapter provides a brief overview of some recent experiments.

Finland

Most of these programs started in just the last year or two. But the current wave of interest in UBI pilots goes back a few years earlier than that, to 2017. In that year, Finland launched what the journalist and UBI advocate Dylan Matthews called a "hugely exciting" experiment on the UBI.[1] Researchers hoped to issue monthly payments of up to roughly 1,000 euros to 10,000 participants over the course of a two-year period. The idea was to test different forms of UBI—a full basic income, a partial basic income, and a NIT—in order to discern how the differences between them influenced outcomes like employment and well-being.

Unfortunately, in what should by now be a familiar story, the ambitions of researchers were quickly put in check by economic and political constraints. The Finnish government was unwilling to provide a budget large enough to cover the wide-ranging set of experiments envisioned by researchers. And, on top of that, a growing number of Finns were becoming concerned with the unconditionality of a UBI (here meaning its lack of a work requirement).[2] Originally, Finland's center-right government had been attracted to the UBI as a way of *reducing* unemployment, by minimizing the perverse incentives of the existing system of unemployment insurance (see chapter 26 for a general discussion of these unintended consequences). But many Finns wondered, if the goal is to get people back to work, then why not make the basic income conditional on employment or an active attempt to obtain employment?

Ultimately the Finnish experiment wound up focusing on a much smaller and more narrowly defined group—2,000 individuals who were already receiving conditional unemployment benefits from the government—and with a significantly smaller payment of 560 Euros instead of 1,000. The results of the experiment showed little effect on labor market participation, though recipients did report higher levels of subjective well-being.[3]

Utrecht, Netherlands

Another study took place in the Dutch city of Utrecht between 2018 and 2019. Once again, experimenters focused on what happened when a portion of individuals receiving the normal conditional unemployment insurance were instead given unconditional assistance. And once again, researchers found a modest positive effect on employment. Other effects were harder to measure, especially due to the small size of the groups. The entire experiment included only 752 people, divided into four treatment groups.

Stockton, California

In 2019, the city of Stockton, California, launched a UBI pilot under which 125 residents would receive $500 per month for twenty-four months. The project, spearheaded by Mayor Michael Tubbs, was labeled the "Stockton Economic Empowerment Demonstration," and was privately funded by donors interested in showcasing the effectiveness of a UBI. As such it was less a social scientific experiment aimed at the gathering and analysis of data than it was a "demonstration" aimed at furthering a UBI politically.

Nevertheless, the project did yield some interesting results, one of which was that individuals receiving the benefit actually worked more than those who did not. This result surprised many observers, especially because in this experiment the benefits were not replacing conditional benefits but merely being added on top of them. One possible explanation, offered by the experimenters, is that "the $500 removed material barriers to full time employment and created capacity for goal setting and risk taking, once basic needs like food and utilities were covered."[4] In other words, sometimes poverty itself can be an obstacle to finding a job, and a UBI can increase employment by removing some of those obstacles. Recipients also showed lower levels of anxiety and depression than those in the control group.

United States

Many of the individuals involved in the Stockton project are now working together in an organization called Mayors for a Guaranteed Income (MGI). MGI seeks to promote UBI experiments in cities across the United States, and currently has around forty such programs in operation. One such program in Santa Clara, California, focuses on children transitioning out of the foster care system, offering them $1,000 per month for one year. Another, in Oakland, California, initially planned to run a UBI limited to people of color, but that condition was dropped after it generated significant backlash on social media. Denver, Colorado, is running a program focused on helping the city's homeless population. And Cambridge, Massachusetts, has a program focused on single caretaker households. You can find out more about MGI's current programs on their website.[5]

Finally, in 2022, California launched the country's first state-funded UBI (second if you count Alaska's), called the California Guaranteed Income Pilot Program, which will award more than $25 million in grant funding to seven different UBI pilot programs across the state. The pilots provide direct monthly cash payments ranging from $600 to $1,200, which will be given to at least 1,975 Californians, with a special focus on young adults transitioning out of the state's foster care program and pregnant women.

37

HOW MUCH CAN WE REALLY LEARN ABOUT A BASIC INCOME FROM PILOT PROGRAMS?

People look to the experiments and pilot programs we've described in this part for information about what a UBI would look like in practice. The idea is to try different versions of a UBI on a small, local scale so we can see what works and what doesn't. With that information in hand, we can then make adjustments before scaling up to the state or federal level.

In theory, pilot programs can provide us with a lot of useful information. For example, we should be able to learn how people spend the money they're given, how a UBI affects people's willingness to work, and how it affects various other longer-term outcomes like physical health, psychological well-being, and educational achievement.

As we have seen in the previous chapters, the results of these programs have generally been encouraging for supporters of a UBI. Most pilots have shown that a UBI does not significantly decrease labor market participation (and in some cases actually increases it), that recipients spend the money responsibly, and that the money has a significant and sometimes long-lasting positive effect on the quality of their lives.

Nevertheless, there are limits to what we can learn from UBI pilots.[1] Some of these limits are specific to particular programs and rooted in various flaws or idiosyncrasies in the way they were designed or executed. Other limitations, however, are more fundamental, and are rooted in issues that will affect *any* pilot program, past, present, or future.

Figuring out how people spend the money they're given with a UBI, for instance, is more difficult than it seems. Some programs, like the Stockton Economic Empowerment Demonstration, give people money on a debit card. This allows researchers to track anything that is purchased directly with the card. But since the program also allowed participants to withdraw some of the money in cash, researchers had to rely on participants to tell them what they spent the rest of the money on.

A deeper problem stems from the fact that money is fungible. Suppose an individual normally spends $100 per month on alcohol and $400 on other groceries. If she receives $100 from a UBI, it would be possible for her to buy $200 worth of alcohol with her own non-UBI money, and use the $100 UBI to make up the resulting deficit in her grocery budget. This would make it appear as though she wasn't using any of her UBI on alcohol, even though the UBI enabled her to double the amount of money she spent on it.

(To be clear, we're not saying that people *would* spend their UBI on alcohol. The point is just that the fungible nature of money makes it difficult or impossible for researchers to know how a UBI changes recipients' overall spending, and how it affects their consumption of so-called vice goods like alcohol.)

Another problem stems from the short time-span of most UBI pilots. Most of these programs last for just one year, or two years at most. But this makes it difficult to get an accurate sense of how a permanent UBI would affect people in different ways, including their willingness to work. Few people will quit their job if they're told they're going to receive $1,000 per month for a year. But offering people $1,000 per year for the rest of their lives is a different matter. It is not unreasonable to expect that a larger number of people would choose to exit the labor market under the latter proposal than under the former.

The way in which pilot programs are funded presents another challenge. Many pilot programs are funded by private money. But a permanent, large-scale program would almost certainly be funded by a mix of taxation and consolidation of existing programs. Because the costs of a UBI are potentially significant, taxes might have to be raised quite a bit and/or several major programs might have to be cut in order to fund it (see chapter 12). In essence, then, privately funded pilot programs are highlighting the benefits of a UBI without any of the costs. They therefore provide a lopsided estimate of the *net* value of a permanent UBI.

In some ways, however, pilot programs might also *underestimate* the benefits of a UBI. As we have discussed, many supporters of a UBI see it as a policy with the potential to radically transform the structure of capitalist society: to change the ways that individuals relate to each other, to their jobs, and to the natural environment. But such transformative outcomes will never appear in a pilot where only a small portion of a city's residents receive a UBI for a short period of time. Small-scale pilots can potentially demonstrate the effects of a UBI on individuals and households, but they are much less well-suited to demonstrating the potential community-wide effects of a UBI. Some of these effects can show up in saturation-type experiments, such as the MINCOME experiment (chapter 34) and the current experiment in Kenya (chapter 35). But the smaller-scale pilots currently being run in the United States miss them altogether.

Part 5

ADVANTAGES

38

COULD A BASIC INCOME HELP US DEAL WITH INCREASING AUTOMATION AND ARTIFICIAL INTELLIGENCE?

So far, we've focused a lot on some of the nuts and bolts issues surrounding a UBI—what it would look like, how it compares to existing programs, and the details of past experiments and current pilots. Let's turn now to what supporters of a UBI hope it will achieve.

One of the most popular arguments for a UBI today is based on concerns about "technological unemployment." The basic idea is that advances in artificial intelligence (AI) and technology will enable machines to do jobs that only humans used to be able to do. Today machines can already drive cars and take your order at a restaurant. And recently released projects such as ChatGPT and DALL-E have stunned the world with their capacity to engage in sophisticated conversation, fix errors in programming code, and even create original works of art. What else will AI be able to do in the future? What *won't* it be able to do?

The worry is that the more that machines can do, the less work will be left for human beings. Machines don't get tired, or distracted, or drunk on the job. And at a certain point of technological development, they're simply going to be a lot cheaper than paying human workers. So, what's going to happen to all our jobs?

This idea was one of the central messages of Andrew Yang's 2020 campaign for the US presidency, and the core of his argument for a

UBI which he called the "Freedom Dividend." Here's what his campaign website said about the issue:

> By 2015, automation had already destroyed four million manufacturing jobs, and the smartest people in the world now predict that a third of all working Americans will lose their job to automation in the next 12 years . . .
>
> As technology improves, workers will be able to stop doing the most dangerous, repetitive, and boring jobs. This should excite us, but if Americans have no source of income—no ability to pay for groceries, buy homes, save for education, or start families with confidence—then the future could be very dark . . .
>
> The Freedom Dividend—funded by a simple Value Added Tax—would guarantee that all Americans benefit from automation, not just big companies.[1]

So, how much of a problem is technological unemployment? And is a UBI the right policy to address it?

As to the first question, there is little evidence at the present time to suggest that AI is destroying jobs, on net. AI creates job *disruption*, but not job *destruction*.[2] In other words, new technologies enable some jobs that used to be done by people to be done by machines instead. But the people who are replaced generally don't just sit on the unemployment rolls. They find other work to do. Overall employment remains steady, despite the "churning" of people moving from one sort of job to another.

Labor-saving innovation is, of course, nothing new. Technological and scientific developments in agriculture, for instance, reduced the number of people working in that sector in the United States from 11 million in 1910 to just over 2 million in 2019, despite massive population growth in the interim.[3] The invention of the automobile destroyed the horse-and-buggy industry. The development of the internet destroyed travel agencies. And yet, here we are. Still working.

But maybe this time is different. AI is, to be sure, a far more radically transformative technology than anything we have ever witnessed. In particular, the *adaptivity* of AI means that its applications are not limited to one particular task or function. We haven't yet seen the evidence of job loss from AI. But maybe that's just because we're in the early stages of the revolution.

Whether AI is radically transformative or merely disruptive, there is an argument to be made for a UBI in either case. If AI really does portend the end of work, then robots are going to do for us everything we used to need humans to do. And that means that almost everything we want will be much, much cheaper. A world full of smart (and hopefully obedient!) robots will be a tremendously wealthy world, and a UBI can help to ensure that that wealth is shared fairly, and not simply captured by whoever happens to own all the robots.

If, on the other hand, AI turns out to be more like globalization—a phenomenon that destroys some jobs and creates others, leaving us generally better off—then a UBI can still be useful. In this scenario, a UBI can help ease the transition for workers who lose their jobs by providing them with the financial resources to relocate, retrain, or otherwise take the time to get back on their feet. Under these circumstances, a UBI wouldn't necessarily need to be big enough to live on permanently. It just needs to be big enough to get by on for a while, until the next job comes around.

Overall, the emphasis on technological unemployment by UBI advocates is probably overstated. Technological unemployment might be a big problem at some point in the future. But it's far from the *only* thing that workers have to worry about, and it's certainly not the most imminent. There are other good reasons to take a UBI seriously, even if we put the issue of technological employment aside altogether. Let's take a look at some of those other reasons now.

39

COULD A BASIC INCOME END POVERTY?

Poverty and inequality remain stubbornly intractable. Even in a country as wealthy as the United States, the Census Bureau estimates that approximately 1 in 10 people—and 1 in 6 children—live in poverty.[1] Around the world, the World Bank estimates that the proportion of people living in poverty is roughly 1 in 12.[2]

Could a UBI end poverty? Many advocates tout UBI as a radically simple way to do so. Andy Stern trumpets that his proposed UBI of $12,000 per adult per year would "end poverty" and help Americans achieve the "life that you want for yourself and your family."[3] Andrew Yang claims one goal of the Freedom Dividend is to "End poverty in the most direct manner possible: giving people money."[4] And Facebook co-founder and Obama advisor Chris Hughes pitches his plan as a way to lift 20 million people out of poverty and provide "economic opportunity to the middle class."[5]

At first, this sounds plausible. If poverty and inequality stem from a lack of money, won't simply giving people money eliminate them? Well, no. As much as we wish it were otherwise, a basic income cannot *eliminate* either poverty or inequality—but it can *reduce* them.

Consider poverty (we'll address inequality in the next chapter). As an initial matter, whether a UBI can end poverty depends in part on what one means by "ending poverty." Does it mean exceeding official measures of poverty, which are, of course, arbitrary? Or does it mean exceeding a normatively acceptable standard of living, and if so, what is that level? Ensuring that nobody faces life-threatening danger from hunger and lack of shelter? Or that everyone has enough to meet basic needs such as food, clothing, shelter, and a few extras like a cellphone at some level of comfort without worry? Or something in the middle? Some government measures nod to this difference; in the United States, for example, the Census Bureau measures both "poverty" and "deep poverty."

A UBI can more easily make a big dent in eradicating life-threatening, constantly starvation-inducing poverty (similar to what deep poverty measures) than in eliminating the grinding crush of worrying about whether you can pay the electric bill and still feed your kids something other than rice before the next paycheck. In that sense, a UBI in the developing world—where even a low level of benefits has a tremendous impact—can do *a lot* to end life-threatening poverty at a realistically affordable price. GiveDirectly's program in Kenya, for example, provides recipients with just 75 cents per day. But in the developed world, our hunch is that most UBI proponents who talk about ending poverty have a higher bar than merely "avoiding death and disaster," which in turn makes it harder for a UBI to clear that bar—and makes the UBI itself more expensive to fund.

Working on that hunch, let's focus on official measures of poverty in developed countries. In the abstract, a polity could just set the size of a UBI so that the UBI (plus any traditional welfare-type transfers) exceeded its official poverty measure. This would, as a definitional matter, end or dramatically lower poverty—in theory. Why only in theory? Cost. To illustrate, the US Census Bureau uses a variety of measures of poverty. The first, which we'll refer to as the official poverty line, was $13,590 for a single adult and $27,750 for a family of four in the contiguous United States in 2022.[6] This measure is arbitrary—it's just three times the cost of a "minimum food diet," and does not reflect regional variations or individual differences in needs such as health care. Deep poverty is half that ($6,795 for a single adult and $13,875 for a family of four in 2022).[7]

A UBI of $500 per month appears to get a single adult almost halfway out of poverty and almost entirely out of deep poverty. A $1,000-per-month UBI appears to lift them out of poverty almost entirely, and puts them well above the deep poverty threshold. (Note that these comparisons are true even if the UBI is of the UBI-minus variety.) Whether a UBI vaults a family above the official line will depend on whether it is paid only to adults, or also to children.

On this point, however, it is important to note one nuance in determining whether someone is above or below the poverty line. At least in the United States, in calculating someone's income to compare it to the official poverty line, not all inflows currently count. But if the point of a UBI is to move someone above the poverty line, it would presumably count toward the income used to determine poverty status. A UBI that replaced uncountable benefits (i.e., a UBI-minus), could appear to lift people above the poverty line without materially changing their well-being. To illustrate, consider *Alexia*, whose wages for a few months' work are $10,000 and who receives $2,000 in unemployment compensation after she is laid off, $3,000 in food stamps, and $2,000 in tax credits. Currently, *Alexia* would include the unemployment compensation but not the in-kind welfare benefits and tax credits when determining whether her income is above or below the poverty line. For that purpose, *Alexia*'s income would be $12,000. Replacing the excludable food stamps and tax credits with a UBI-minus that counted toward income for the purposes of measuring poverty would raise her "official" income to $17,000 but not materially improve her well-being. And if benefits such as SNAP and the EITC that favor families with children were eliminated in favor of a UBI that did not include children, the family of four would likely be worse off (see chapter 53).

For our purposes, a more precise measure of poverty is the supplemental poverty measure, or SPM. The SPM is higher, but includes inflows such as tax credits and welfare benefits when comparing someone's income to it. The 2021 SPM for a two-adult, two-child family of four that doesn't own a home was $31,453. Giving this family a UBI of $500 per month per person that included children would provide them with an annual income of $24,000, which is still several thousand dollars a year below the official SPM; a $1,000-per-month UBI to adults only yields the same result. In contrast, a $1,000-per-month UBI to young and old alike would lift this family above the SPM line. As we discussed in part 2, however, this sum is unrealistically large.

Note that these calculations assume a UBI-minus that replaces existing benefits. A UBI-plus that supplements existing welfare programs instead of replacing them could more easily lift a family above official poverty measures, of course, but would also be so expensive as to be unrealistic.

Circling back to our original question, a *realistically-sized* UBI won't lift this family out of poverty. But even a $500-per-month UBI can make a substantial difference in their well-being (see chapters 28 and 51) and make it much, much easier for this family to raise themselves above the SPM. Earning an additional $7,000 per year—which works out to an additional $583 per month—is not entirely unrealistic in most instances. This would require one of the adults to work approximately twenty hours per week at the federal minimum wage of $7.25 per hour, and half that in states with a $15-per-hour minimum wage. A UBI can therefore make a dent in poverty, even if it can't end it all by itself.

40

COULD A BASIC INCOME REDUCE INEQUALITY?

Like poverty, inequality remains a stubbornly intractable problem, and in fact, has grown tremendously in the last few decades. For example, a recent Pew Research Report finds that income inequality in the United States has increased by about 20% since 1980.[1] Wealth inequality is even more striking; the share of wealth held by the wealthiest 1% of families is reaching levels not seen since the 1920s! And at the same time, rates of social mobility—earning more than your parents or moving up the income distribution—have been dropping.[2]

How might a UBI impact inequality? Here, it's important to distinguish between inequality of outcomes and inequality of opportunity. Looking just at the distribution of income among individuals focuses on outcomes. A UBI can make only a small dent in this type of inequality. In 2019, for example, median household income was almost $68,000—even a $1,000-per-month UBI that included children wouldn't reach the median income! And at the top, the mean income of the top 20% was over $250,000 and almost $450,000 for the top 5% of households in 2020.[3] In theory, of course, a UBI coupled with additional structural changes—such as a much more steeply progressive tax system—might be able to minimize *ex post* income and wealth inequality, but that topic is far beyond our scope. For our purposes, the take-away is that a realistically sized UBI wouldn't do much to close the gap in equality of outcomes.

Even so, what a UBI can do is help *minimize*—but not *eliminate*—inequality of opportunity. Setting aside whether a just world also requires equality of outcomes, most would agree that a poor child should have the same opportunities as a rich child to develop her talents and abilities and chart her own life path. Yet material resources available at birth undeniably influence a person's ability to do this.

Starting even before birth, financial hardship can negatively impact later life outcomes—studies suggest that poor nutrition and maternal stress while a child is in utero adversely affect outcomes into adulthood.[4] As discussed elsewhere, research from various cash transfer programs have found associations between such programs and reduced maternal stress, higher birth-weights, and fewer preterm births—which point to one way a UBI can help give children from lower-income households a more equal starting point.

During childhood, children who grow up in families with more resources have better nutrition, greater access to medical care and education, higher quality child care, and so on. A UBI can't eliminate these advantages full stop. Wealthier families will always be able to pay for tutors, private schools or houses in neighborhoods with better schools, expensive music lessons, and enrichment trips to Europe.

A UBI can't change that. But for a poor family, a UBI might keep the lights on while a child does homework, help a family buy a computer, pay for basic after-school activities, or allow an overworked parent to spend more time with his or her child. And as discussed elsewhere, cash transfers to families with children are associated with numerous benefits that influence later outcomes—increased childhood nutrition, higher test scores, and additional years of schooling. Studies have also shown associations between cash transfers and later outcomes themselves, such as lower rates of incarceration and higher incomes as adults.

All of which suggest that a UBI can help create a more equal starting point. What happens after, however, is still up for grabs. Bad luck will befall some; others will make poor choices (despite the fact most people will not waste their UBI; see chapter 51). People have different natural endowments in terms of intelligence, physical attributes, and drive. A UBI can't eliminate poverty or guarantee either equality of outcomes or perfect equality of opportunity, but it can minimize the role that the chance financial circumstances of birth play in one's life.

41

WOULD A BASIC INCOME BE SIMPLER AND MORE EFFICIENT?

To many UBI supporters, its simplicity and efficiency are key advantages. As we discussed throughout part 3, providing an automatic, no-strings-attached cash transfer via a single agency is simpler than administering numerous in-kind and restricted programs, each with its own eligibility requirements, scattered among multiple agencies. This simplicity yields several efficiencies at both the provider and beneficiary levels.[1] This is especially true when considering a UBI that would replace current welfare programs, although the comparative advantages—especially to recipients—hold if a UBI is layered atop such programs.

At the provider level, a UBI that replaces the array of existing welfare programs would likely reduce the size and expense of government bureaucracy. Consider the following. In the United States, thirty-three different federal housing assistance programs are operated by four different cabinet departments—including the Department of Energy. Twenty-one food or food-purchasing assistance programs are run by three cabinet departments and one independent agency. And twenty-seven cash or general-assistance programs are operated by six different cabinet departments and five other independent agencies.[2] Replacing this web with one streamlined program would presumably reduce administrative costs, especially given the relative ease of distributing cash instead of in-kind benefits. Similarly, cash payments are less susceptible to interest group lobbying; consider the jockeying that almost certainly occurs among providers for contracts for in-kind benefits or to be included in lists of "acceptable" purchases.

A UBI also avoids recipient-level inefficiencies, given that individuals often find ways to turn in-kind benefits into cash. Consider reports of a soda "black market" in rural Appalachia. According to Kevin Williamson, some SNAP recipients buy large quantities of soda that they then resell for cash at steeply discounted values—as much as 50 cents on the dollar, meaning that they have given up, say, $400 of in-kind benefits for $200 cash.[3] For these individuals, asserting their autonomy comes at a steep price; there is also a cost to the government in that half the value of the benefits have been captured by black market soda purchasers.

Moreover, consolidating the work of numerous agencies into one means that recipients will no longer have to spend time and energy navigating multiple welfare programs, each with their own forms, many requiring office visits, and which often have conflicting eligibility requirements. Reducing the cost to beneficiaries leaves them more time for work or family. In some cases, this may even mean that a previously unemployed individual has enough time and energy left to find a job!

UBI detractors argue that these efficiency concerns are overstated. First, while it might be fairly easy for SNAP recipients to exchange soda for other goods, it is much harder to sell other in-kind benefits—say Medicaid or government housing—on a secondary market. Second, there may be pragmatic reasons to prefer in-kind benefits. For some goods and services, the state may enjoy economies of scale and/or other advantages. Take medical care. Several studies suggest that Medicaid offers access to services that are comparable in quality to those available on the private health care market, but at a much lower cost.[4]

Finally, those who wish to help only "deserving" individuals may prefer in-kind or restricted benefits as a screening mechanism. This argument assumes that in-kind benefits are lower quality and come with a certain amount of stigma. If so, then only those who truly cannot support themselves will settle for such goods; those who can work to afford higher quality goods will do so. Similarly, the stigma and hassle necessary to obtain benefits—by visiting multiple agencies and navigating multiple application processes—might serve a similar screening function by discouraging people who do not truly need assistance from applying. It is far from clear, however, that these hurdles will effectively screen out the undeserving.

In fact, those who are better able to clear these hurdles and navigate the welfare bureaucracy are likely better able to navigate the labor market. And vice versa. These hurdles, then, may inadvertently screen out those who are least able to fend for themselves in the labor market and who are therefore more deserving of aid.

42

WOULD A BASIC INCOME ENHANCE AUTONOMY AND DIGNITY?

People who depend on welfare often feel it to be a degrading experience. It's never easy to have to depend on someone else to provide for your basic necessities, or the support of your family. It is even more difficult when obtaining that support requires submitting to an intrusive bureaucratic process in which the most personal details of your life are scrutinized in an atmosphere of mistrust.

Some have argued that a UBI would avoid this sort of paternalistic and demeaning treatment, for two reasons. First, because a UBI is a cash grant, it leaves it to each individual beneficiary to determine his or her most urgent needs. In-kind benefits such as food stamps or housing vouchers are premised on the idea that the government knows what people really need better than they themselves do. But suppose that what somebody needs right now is not groceries but to pay an overdue cell phone bill, or to pay for public transportation? Or what if they don't actually need *anything* right now but would like to save for the future? A cash grant allows individuals to make their own decisions about how to use their benefit, and in doing so it treats them with a kind of respect that is often lacking from alternative forms of welfare.

Second, because a UBI is a non-discretionary grant, individuals are spared the indignity of having to demonstrate their worthiness to a government bureaucrat. Every restriction that is placed on welfare eligibility is another hoop that recipients have to jump through. At various times, in various places, welfare recipients have had their homes inspected (to ensure that they are not being financially supported by another member of their household), have been spied on (to ensure they're really trying to find a job), and forced to pee in a cup (to ensure they're not on drugs). Distinguishing between the "deserving" and the "undeserving" poor might sound innocent enough in theory, but in practice figuring out whether a person's misfortune is due to bad luck or bad choices is a complicated matter that cannot be settled without significant intrusion in people's personal lives.

A separate concern is that officials charged with making these distinctions will inevitably bring their own biases and value judgments to the process. This will result in uneven implementation, in tension with the rule of law. Relatedly, the success of individuals in convincing government officials that they are unable to work may turn on factors that are orthogonal to work ability. Or, worse yet, the individuals who succeed in persuading officials of their inability might be the ones who are in fact most capable of work. As James Greiner and Cassandra Pattanayak suggest, individuals who succeed in enlisting pro bono representation or other legal aid might be "disproportionately worldly."[1] These same individuals also may be the ones most capable of finding and filling jobs. Perversely, the result of screening efforts might be to screen in the least deserving and screen out the most.

43

COULD A BASIC INCOME IMPROVE THE POSITION OF PEOPLE OF COLOR?

Another seemingly intractable problem that America is still struggling with is racial injustice. People of color in the United States face a variety of obstacles ranging from outright bigotry to countless smaller indignities. No single policy could possibly rectify the entire range of injustices and inequities to which people of color are subjected. But there is some reason to believe that a UBI might help.

Some of the clearest manifestations of racial injustice in the United States are economic in nature. In particular, there is a marked "racial wealth gap" and "racial earnings gap" between white households and Black and Hispanic/Latino households. According to one report by the Federal Reserve, "the average Black and Hispanic or Latino households earn about half as much as the average White household and own only about 15 to 20 percent as much net wealth."[1] These gaps are both longstanding and stubbornly persistent. As the authors of another study for the Federal Reserve Bank of Minneapolis note, "no progress has been made in reducing income and wealth inequalities between black and white households over the last 70 years."[2]

Inequalities in wealth exacerbate the damage caused by low or precarious income. The sociologist Alexandra Kilewald puts it this way: "You can think of income as water flowing into your bathtub, whereas wealth is like the water that's sitting in the bathtub. If you have wealth, it can protect you if you lose your job or your house. Wealth is distinctive because it can be used as a cushion, and it can be directly passed down across generations."[3]

Not only can wealth be passed down to future generations directly—it also affects the opportunities open to future generations through its effect on education. In the United States, schools are tied to neighborhoods, which means that sending your child to a good school often means moving into the right neighborhood. Neighborhoods with better schools are in higher demand by parents, driving home prices up and pricing out those families unable to afford the premium. Poorer families are thus locked out of the better schools, which means worse educational opportunities for their children, and lower earnings potential for them in the future.

There has been some interest in using a UBI to target racial wealth and income gaps directly, by limiting the grant exclusively to people of color. The city of Oakland, California, for instance, considered launching a UBI pilot limited exclusively to people of color, but wound up opening the program to all low-income citizens after severe criticism.[4] Atlanta is currently running a UBI pilot limited to Black women. And Community Change President Dorian Warren has proposed what he calls a Universal + Basic Income model, which would implement a UBI with an additional payment to black families as partial reparation for the systematic injustices suffered by African Americans.[5]

But even a race-neutral UBI can be effective in closing the gaps in racial wealth and income. Because people of color are disproportionately represented among the poor in the United States, any program that redistributes wealth from rich to poor will tend to narrow the racial wealth gap. And while the UBI is technically a "universal" grant that everyone receives, virtually all proposed programs are designed in a way that leaves the poor net beneficiaries and the rich net contributors to the program (see chapters 8 and 9).

Moreover, because the UBI is universal, it avoids the stigmatization associated with traditional means-tested welfare programs, a stigmatization that has disproportionately affected people of color (think of stereotypical images of "welfare queens"). It also blocks the temptation to make welfare harder to get in order to deny access to people of color—a temptation to which, as research has shown, state legislators have all too often yielded.[6] For example, when Nixon proposed a kind of federal Negative Income Tax in 1969, some of the strongest opposition came from Southern states. Legislators from those states feared that a federal UBI would undermine their ability to control black citizens and maintain racial hierarchies. Discretionary state welfare programs could be manipulated to serve racist ends; a federally controlled non-discretionary program could not.

Another intangible benefit of a UBI, as we discuss in chapter 46, is that it gives people the power to say no. Despite much racial progress over the past few decades, many racial minorities still feel that they must endure on-the-job slights and harassment that others don't. A UBI can provide a cushion so that they can speak up without fear, or find a job where they feel more respected.

UBI cannot solve all the problems faced by people of color. But to the extent that inequalities of income and wealth are linked to a variety of other inequalities in education, health, exposure to violent crime, and so on, as well as to the extent that a UBI can help to shrink the size of those gaps, it might be a step in the right direction.

44

HOW WILL A BASIC INCOME AFFECT FAMILIES?

The well-being of the family as an institution is also critically important to the health of a society. We've talked elsewhere about how a UBI is an individual benefit (chapter 13), whether children and seniors would receive a UBI (chapters 14 and 15), and the benefits of child allowances and tax credits (chapter 28). And in chapter 61, we'll talk about feminism and a UBI. These discussions all touch on the fact that most people, including women, children and seniors, do not live alone. They live in *families*. How would a UBI affect the family as an institution?

One question is whether it would change incentives to get or stay married or to have children. We predict that on net, it wouldn't change the overall number of married couples. The financial stability of a UBI would likely enable some women to leave abusive relationships, a benefit many feminists rightfully trumpet. Less worthy of celebration, it's also possible that some unenthusiastic parents (say, some unmarried fathers) might be less likely to stick around or pay child support if they know their child's other parent is receiving a UBI. These considerations might decrease the number of committed relationships. Offsetting that, however, is that a well-designed UBI would avoid the penalties embedded in many existing programs that currently *discourage* marriage and the combining of households (see chapter 13). So, while some couples will likely decide to end marriages and similar relationships, others will likely decide to start them.

A related question is whether a UBI would affect family size. Charles Murray, for example, excludes children from his UBI proposal on the grounds that including them would encourage poorer adults to have more children. In contrast, he believes that excluding children will make people think twice about having additional children.[1] Ironically, many current welfare programs heavily favor families *with* children, while childless individuals see little or no benefit. Empirical evidence on the extent to which fertility is affected by existing welfare policies is mixed.[2] At the outset, it seems that a UBI given to adults whether or not they have children—even if children also receive one—would incentivize child-bearing less than the current system which often provides childless adults with next-to-nothing.

Why might child-bearing decisions be less responsive than marriage decisions? Well, one can reap many of the benefits of a long-term relationship without actually getting married, making it fairly easy for people to change their behavior in response to marriage penalties. The same can't be said for having children, which suggests that policies designed to reduce family size are less effective. And of course, whether policies should discourage, encourage, or be neutral on family size is a question of values.

What we can be more confident of, however, is that in a variety of ways, a UBI would likely enhance the quality of life of, and decrease conflict and strife in, families that remain together. First, a UBI would decrease stress by providing regular cash, no strings attached. Parents would worry less about finding money to feed their children, or buy them clothes, school supplies, or medicine. With fewer financial stressors, some parents will likely fight less and have fewer distractions. It's hard to see how the quality of life within the family home would not improve with less conflict and stress.

In theory, existing benefit programs ease some of these concerns. But as we've discussed elsewhere, the restricted and conditional nature of these programs has drawbacks. Food stamps can't be used for vitamins or diapers or already-prepared "hot foods" like a roast chicken. Families worry about benefits ending when eligibility runs out, or benefits being irregular due to erratic work schedules. A steady stream of no-strings-attached cash likely eases familial stress in ways these programs do not.

And as we've discussed elsewhere (especially in chapters 28 and 51), giving cash to families appears to help children thrive. Such transfers are associated with—among other measures—higher test scores, staying in school longer, fewer disciplinary incidents, higher birth-weights, fewer pre-term babies, and enhanced nutrition. Improving children's well-being is one of the primary benefits of families.

The unconditional nature of a UBI offers some additional benefits, as well. First, it can give families more time together. Evidence from past NIT experiments in the United States and Canada suggest that to the extent recipients of unconditional cash transfers change their work patterns, it is generally as follows: some new mothers delay re-entry into the workforce, and some primary caregivers work somewhat fewer hours per week. More time at home allows parents to increase time spent with their children, developing human capital by dining together, reading to them, playing games, helping them with homework, and just hanging out. As one researcher commented on the earlier NIT experiments in the United States, "Some of [the work response] came from cutting down hours, say from 65 to 60 hours a week, which doesn't seem like a tragedy."[3]

Additionally, the UBI's unconditional nature enhances autonomy and dignity in a way that likely enhances the family atmosphere. Parents are empowered to say no to dehumanizing jobs, again improving moods with the family. Parents—often mothers—who work at home have more financial autonomy, giving them more of a say in the household. And removing work requirements signals that unpaid labor has value. It is hard to see how daily life within a family doesn't improve when members feel more empowered and respected within and without the household walls, instead of feeling trapped. And although we recognize that those whose view of the family is more traditional may chafe at some of these changes, we believe most will find them positive.

45

HOW WOULD A BASIC INCOME AFFECT COMMUNITIES?

We've now spent a lot of time in this book talking about the ways that a UBI might benefit individuals and families. But some people have also argued that a UBI would produce benefits on a larger, community-wide scale. This argument has been especially prominent among conservative defenders of a UBI, such as Charles Murray. In fact, Murray has argued that the transformative effect of a UBI on America's civic culture would constitute "the most important single contribution of a UBI."[1]

In making this argument, Murray draws on the observations of Alexis de Tocqueville, who in his 19th-century travels in America witnessed a distinctive and beneficial tendency among its citizens to form and join associations. This tendency, Tocqueville believed, had a profound effect on how Americans got things done. "In every case, at the head of any new undertaking, where in France you would find the government or in England some territorial magnate, in the United States you are sure to find an association."[2]

Over the course of the 20th century, however, Federal, state, and local governments have taken on a larger and larger share of the tasks that used to be the purview of private associations. Prior to the New Deal, for instance, "social security" and old age insurance was mostly provided for by various "friendly societies."[3] These societies operated on the principle of mutual aid and collective insurance, with members paying dues during good times and receiving benefits when times got rough. But when the Federal government started providing many of the same benefits for free, friendly societies and other forms of voluntary association were gradually "crowded out" of the social insurance business.

By putting financial resources—and perhaps more free time—back into the hands of communities, a UBI might help empower them to take some of these functions back. This "devolution of responsibility" would be especially pronounced if, as Murray envisions, the UBI would *replace* many functions of the current welfare state, rather than simply be added on top of them.

Murray argues that community-based, private associations have certain advantages over state bureaucracies in dealing with the problems of poverty. Community members are in a better position to know the particular circumstances, needs, and resources available to them than a distant bureaucracy. And private community organizations are more able to experiment with different approaches to solving problems. Government bureaucracies *need* to be constrained by fixed rules and procedures, for reasons of fairness and transparency. There is no space within a bureaucracy for approaches motivated by moral or religious convictions that are not universally shared among the public. In contrast, Murray notes, "not only are private organizations free to combine moral instruction with the help they give, but such moral instruction is often a primary motivation for the people who are doing the work."[4]

Insofar as a UBI would strengthen private associations, Murray argues that this would be good for society and good for individuals and families. It would be good for society by strengthening the affiliations and social capital that such institutions promote, helping to reverse the trend of social isolation that Robert Putnam famously described as "bowling alone."[5] And it would be good for individuals because community associations are more than just a tool for producing a certain outcome. They are an important component of well-being and happiness for people—a source of community and support, and an opportunity to interact with diverse others in pursuit of a common goal.

Of course, it is difficult to know exactly how a UBI would affect communities. As discussed in chapter 37, most of the pilot programs on the UBI have been limited in duration and have covered only a small portion of the entire community. This means that a lot of the larger-scale effects of a UBI—good or bad—simply do not show up in the results of such experiments.

For example, there is a difference between a handful of workers receiving a UBI and *all* workers receiving a UBI. A few workers getting a UBI will not have any effect on the prevailing wage rate. But if all workers receive a UBI, we would expect the supply of labor to decrease somewhat, which in turn should lead to an increase in wages, which in turn should lead to a somewhat larger supply of workers. These and other "equilibrium effects" of a UBI simply don't show up in short-term, small-scale experiments. So, they must remain, for now, a matter of speculation.

46

HOW WOULD A BASIC INCOME AFFECT THE PROBLEM OF "BULLSHIT JOBS"?

Another problem that resonates deeply with much of the public is reflected in the title of a book published in 2018 by the anthropologist David Graeber: *Bullshit Jobs*.[1] Graeber defined a bullshit job as "a form of paid employment that is so completely pointless, unnecessary, or pernicious that even the employee cannot justify its existence even though, as part of the conditions of employment, the employee feels obliged to pretend that this is not the case." And he argued that they were becoming more common.

Graeber's category of bullshit jobs encompassed a wide variety of familiar work—"duct tapers" who apply temporary fixes to deeper structural problems, "task masters" whose sole function seems to be the creation of additional meaningless work, and "goons" who harm or deceive others on behalf of their employer. But even many people who do not fall under one of Graeber's categories nevertheless feel that there is something deeply wrong with their work. For many low-wage workers, the hours are too long, the pay and benefits are too low, and the employment is too precarious. And the problems seem to be getting worse.

Economists have pointed to a number of factors that help to explain the worsening position of workers. Globalization has opened up workers in wealthy countries to competition from cheap labor in the developing world, lowering wages in certain sectors of the economy and eliminating whole categories of jobs elsewhere. Unionization has declined, and the lack of collective bargaining has left workers ill-prepared to claim their share of the profits of increased productivity. Finally, a greater number of individuals find themselves employed in the "gig economy," where future income is difficult to predict, and the legally mandated benefits of full-time employment are unavailable.

How can a UBI help? The answer is a simple application of bargaining theory. A worker with no alternative source of wealth or income to fall back on has little choice but to say "yes" to any demand his or her boss makes. By providing everyone with a predictable stream of income, a UBI would strengthen the negotiating power of workers relative to employers. A UBI gives workers the power to say "no," knowing that they have at least some sort of cushion to fall back on. In an era where many workers no longer have a union to call on for support, a UBI can serve, as Timothy Roscoe Carter put it, as "the ultimate permanent strike fund."[2]

A national UBI could also help to improve the mobility of labor, which is good both for the overall efficiency of the economy and the well-being of individual workers. When you're living paycheck to paycheck, it can be hard to leave your current job in order to find a better one. That can be especially hard if the better job is in another city or state. A UBI can help to cover both the time in between jobs and the costs of relocating.

Finally, a UBI can help individuals to take the time away from work necessary to acquire the education or job-specific training necessary to get a better, higher-paying job. This is especially important now in an era of rapidly expanding occupational licensing. A wide range of jobs, including taxi driving, cosmetology, and even working as a florist, now require a state license which can only be obtained by completing certain specified mandatory training. Obtaining a license to work as a manicurist in the state of Alabama, for example, requires the completion of a whopping 163 days of training![3]

Whether it's paying to relocate, paying to receive training, or paying to have someone watch your children while you leave the home, the lesson is the same. Poverty is often a trap that is difficult to escape. In a wide range of cases, it simply takes money to make money. By providing a base level of income, a UBI can serve as a stepping stone for workers to make big improvements to their working lives. Seen in this light, it's perhaps not surprising that a range of studies have shown that a UBI actually produces an *increase* in employment—an issue that we discuss in part 4 of this book.

COULD A BASIC INCOME HELP US TO ADDRESS ENVIRONMENTAL PROBLEMS?

At first glance, it might not be obvious what a UBI has to do with a final pressing problem, the environment. But it turns out that environmental activists have long been supporters of a basic income. For example, the British Ecology Party included a call for a UBI in its platform as far back as the late 1970s, and today a UBI is part of the platform of the Green Party in the United Kingdom, the United States, and elsewhere. Here is what the US Green Party platform says about a UBI, under the heading of "Economic Justice & Sustainability":

> We call for a universal basic income (sometimes called a guaranteed income, negative income tax, citizen's income, or citizen dividend). This would go to every adult regardless of health, employment, or marital status, in order to minimize government bureaucracy and intrusiveness into people's lives. The amount should be sufficient so that anyone who is unemployed can afford basic food and shelter. State or local governments should supplement that amount from local revenues where the cost of living is high.[1]

Why would environmentalists care about a UBI? The answer is to be found in the green perspective on economic growth. For many environmentalists, the relentless pursuit of economic growth is a serious problem. It is true that growth has led to numerous improvements in human well-being. But environmentalists sometimes argue that capitalism has a tendency to push growth beyond the point at which it makes a meaningful contribution to people's lives. Capitalism drives society toward growth for the sake of growth, regardless of whether it actually makes us better off.

Moreover, that economic growth comes at a significant environmental cost. However efficient markets might be in allocating scarce resources among competing human needs, they nevertheless generally fail to take account of the external cost of human decisions on the broader environment. Air pollution, water pollution, and global climate change are the byproducts of the endless quest for growth. And while government regulation might help to curb some of the worst excesses of this damage, many environmentalists argue that curbing economic growth is the only viable solution in the long run.

Seen from this perspective, the UBI has two advantages—both of which, ironically, are often seen as disadvantages by the majority of observers. The first advantage has to do with the cost of a UBI. Suppose we adopted a relatively generous UBI that required significant new taxation to fund. This additional taxation, many argue, might have the effect of slowing down economic growth. But from an environmentalist perspective, this might actually be a good thing—a feature, not a bug.

Second, some have argued that a UBI will make leisure more attractive than work, at least on the margin—see our discussion of the "income effect" in chapter 49. So, people receiving a UBI might work less and spend more time with their family, or volunteering, or just lounging around the house. To many economists, this is worrisome. But from an environmentalist perspective, this is again a positive good. Less work means less commuting and slower economic growth. As it happens, it also means people will have more time to spend outside, perhaps developing a greater appreciation for the natural environment.

There is one more way in which a UBI is connected with environmental concerns. This has to do with one of the oldest arguments for a UBI, rooted in the idea that natural resources belong to *everyone*, not just whichever individual, or group, happens to capture them first. We mentioned this argument briefly in chapter 2 in our discussion of Thomas Paine, but we'll return to it more fully in chapter 63 on libertarianism.

Part 6

OBJECTIONS

48

WOULD A BASIC INCOME BE TOO EXPENSIVE?

We've just talked about some of the benefits of a UBI, and way back in part 2, we talked about how much a UBI would cost and ways to fund it. A valid concern—even for folks convinced of a UBI's benefits—is whether a UBI is affordable.

Like so many questions discussed in this book . . . it depends. A small UBI financed entirely by a carbon tax or financial transactions tax would likely strike very few—if any—as "too expensive." And as we've discussed, even fairly small cash transfers are associated with noticeable improvements in people's well-being (see part 4).

But as we saw in chapter 11, the net cost of a $500 or $1,000-per-month UBI is likely over a trillion dollars—even for a UBI-minus that replaced numerous existing programs and expenditures. And as we discussed in chapter 12, raising enough new revenue to cover a UBI of this size would likely require more-than-minimal taxes, such as a VAT in the 10% range or a surtax on income in the 7–9% range plus some combination of other, smaller, taxes. So yes, funding the type of UBI that captures most people's imaginations is expensive, even when it replaces many existing programs. And funding a UBI-plus that supplements existing transfer programs would be even more expensive.

Is it *too* expensive? Well, that depends on the UBI's size, plus your tolerance for taxation and your preferences for redistribution. Elsewhere, one of us has estimated that the cost of a $500 per-person per-month UBI that replaced most current welfare programs in the United States would be roughly 7% of GDP.[1] Government spending in the United States is currently around 38% of GDP, compared to

49% of GDP in Norway and 50% in Sweden. A $500-per-month UBI would keep the ratio of US government spending to GDP below Nordic levels, while a $1,000-per-month UBI would vault us ahead of Denmark (55%) and just behind Finland and France, both of whom clock in at 57%. We are doubtful that the United States is willing to become one of the most heavily taxed countries, if not the most heavily taxed, to fund such a large UBI.

But whether we are willing to increase taxes by a noticeable but not enormous amount to fund a medium-sized UBI is an open question. For those who believe that a UBI's benefits (such as the increases in well-being from transferring cash to families with children) outweigh its costs, then a UBI is well worth it. But for those inclined to be skeptical of a UBI at the outset, we suspect that any cost would be too great.

49

WOULD A BASIC INCOME DISCOURAGE PEOPLE FROM WORKING?

After cost, one of the most common objections to a UBI is that it will discourage people from working. How valid is that objection?

Although it's hard to say for sure, any realistically sized UBI probably would not encourage primary breadwinners to drop permanently out of the labor force in large numbers. Depending on how generous it is, however, a UBI might lead some people to stop working. It might also lead to a decline in total hours worked (without anyone dropping out of the labor force) by reducing overtime hours and encouraging some workers, such as teenagers and new mothers, to delay entering or reentering the workforce. This would be especially true for a UBI layered atop existing transfer programs, which is the context in which we'd likely see the most adverse impact on employment.

However, such impacts would likely be less true for a UBI-minus that replaced many current benefits. Why? Well, in thinking about how such a UBI would affect people's willingness to work, the key question to ask is: compared to what? Compared to a world without any redistribution at all, giving people money for nothing would probably lead to a net decrease in overall employment. But that's not the world we live in. For a UBI-minus, the better baseline is our existing welfare system, which already discourages work in a number of ways. Compared to that baseline, a UBI-minus might actually encourage lower-income workers to work *more*.

To see why, it is important to understand a distinction economists draw between two ways that a UBI might influence people's willingness to work: an "income effect" and a "substitution effect." An "income effect" occurs when a change in income—becoming richer or poorer—affects one's willingness to work. All else being equal, leisure is a good that people tend to "buy" more of as their income increases. The more money you get from the government, the more likely you are to use some of this money to support yourself while you work fewer hours and relax. Therefore, because of the income effect, a UBI might lead to some decrease in either hours worked or labor force participation among lower-income individuals, just as most people assume it would.

However, a UBI-minus would have another, not-so-obvious effect. This effect, called the "substitution effect," leads people to work *more* when the opportunity cost for leisure is increased. When marginal tax rates on labor decrease, your after-tax earnings go up. It therefore becomes more expensive to take time off from work and people are more likely to substitute work for leisure. Because of the substitution effect, low-income individuals might actually work *more* under a basic income that replaced existing programs.

Why? The key here is to recognize that most current welfare systems "phase out" benefits in a way that has the same effect as taxing the labor income of welfare recipients. Imagine that you are a SNAP recipient whose benefits decrease by $35 for each $100 of income you have.[1] This acts exactly like a 35% tax on your earnings: even though you gross $100, your net benefit, after accounting for a drop in SNAP benefits, is only $65.

When you combine all the phase-outs from existing anti-poverty programs, a tenth of households at or just above the poverty line face implicit marginal rates over 65%, meaning that they net only $35 of each additional $100 of earned income. The average marginal rate for this group is 34%.[2] And at the extreme end, some programs take away your benefits altogether once your income hits a cliff-like ceiling. For example, in 2022, someone on disability who earned more than $1,350 per month could lose up to $841 all at once when her income reached $1,351.[3] Would you work an extra hour in that case? A well-designed UBI can be structured to phase out more gently than existing welfare programs and to avoid cliff effects, which would make work more financially rewarding than under the current system. If so, the net effect of a UBI on low-wage workers' willingness to work would likely be minimal.

Data from other cash-transfer programs and a series of experiments in the 1970s and 1980s can also be helpful in understanding the likely effect of a UBI on employment. For example, a study comparing families with children who received the Eastern Band of Cherokee Indians casino disbursements with similar families not receiving disbursements found no significant effect on labor supply for parents. Studies of the Alaska Permanent Dividend Fund have also found no significant effect on labor-force participation and a minimal effect, if any, on hours worked.[4] Given that these programs are neither funded by taxes nor do they replace existing programs, they do not tell us anything about the substitution effect of a UBI. But they do suggest that at the low-end, concerns about a negative income effect may be overblown. This is especially true when those concerns are raised about a UBI-minus, since the casino payments and Alaska dividends more closely resemble a UBI-plus.

Evidence from the US Negative Income Tax (NIT) experiments is more equivocal. We have a lot more to say about these experiments in chapter 33, but for now, the important point is that these experiments seemed to show that implementing a transfer scheme like a UBI led people to work less. Moreover, this reduction in work was greatest (about a 4% drop) where the benefits were most generous (in the Seattle/Denver locations).

How this finding should be interpreted, however, is somewhat complicated. In particular, there are three important qualifications to the general finding above. The first stems from the fact that the NIT experiments had to rely on individuals' self-reports of their income. Because participants received more money from the government the lower their earned income was, this created a perverse incentive for individuals to under-report their actual income and hours worked. For this reason, the official results of the experiments probably *over-state* the extent to which the NIT caused a reduction in actual hours worked. Second, the NIT experiments contained very steep phase-outs, much like the current welfare system. Most current proposals phase out more gently and would therefore increase the financial return to labor compared to the current welfare system. Both of these qualifications suggest that the results of the NIT experiments might not be as bad for supporters of a UBI as some critics have thought.

There is a third qualification, however, to which critics of a UBI can still point. Even if the NIT experiments did not lead to a significant decrease in work, this does not mean that a full-fledged UBI would not do so. This is because the NIT experiments were *temporary*, whereas a UBI would be *permanent*. Very few people will stop working altogether if they are told that they are going to receive cash from the government for the next twelve months. Whether they would do so if they were told that they will receive cash for the rest of their lives is a different matter. A permanent basic income would create very different incentives than a temporary experiment, and could lead a larger number of people to work less, or to stop working altogether. That said, behavioral responses to the Alaska Permanent Fund suggest that this fear might also be overblown, as a recent study found that rates of overall labor force participation did not noticeably change after its introduction. Rates of part-time work increased, although it is not clear whether this was due to full-time workers shifting to part-time work (thereby working less) or non-workers entering the part-time labor force (thereby working more).[5]

Figuring out the extent to which a UBI would cause people to work less is a complicated economic matter. But even putting that question to the side, there is a difficult philosophical question here too: would causing people to work less really be all that bad? Unlike the economic question, which is about measuring the effects of different kinds of policy interventions, this question is about *values*. How important do we think it is for people to work in the paid labor market—both for their own good and for the good of the society they live in? Is work a means to an end, or an end in itself? In all likelihood, our answers to these questions will be complicated, and context-dependent. There is probably a difference, for instance, between how we feel about someone who drops out of work to spend her time surfing the beaches of Malibu and someone who takes some extra time off from work to spend with her newborn child. We turn to these questions in the next chapter.

50

WHY SUPPORT PEOPLE WHO COULD WORK BUT CHOOSE NOT TO?

Another frequent objection to the UBI stems from the fact that it is *unconditional*. That means that people are eligible to receive a UBI whether they're working or not, and even whether they're *willing* to work or not.

To many people, this seems wrong. It's one thing for the government to provide support for people who are genuinely unable to support themselves. But it seems quite different to use taxpayer money to support people who *could* provide for themselves but choose not to. The former class of people are the *deserving poor*—those who truly deserve society's help, since their poverty is no fault of their own. The latter group of people, according to this way of thinking, are the *undeserving poor*, whose poverty is rooted in their own choices.

This sounds like a very conservative objection to the UBI, and indeed many who find this worry compelling do identify with the political right. But a very similar sort of objection has been expressed by some prominent thinkers on the political left. John Rawls, who was probably the most influential liberal philosopher of the 20th century, set out his view of social justice in his 1971 book, *A Theory of Justice*.[1] That view, at its root, was based on an understanding of society as a "cooperative venture for mutual advantage." In other words, society involves us working together to achieve our common aims, and justice is largely a matter of how to distribute the proceeds of that shared effort.

On this view, social justice is rooted in a deeper commitment to *reciprocity*—the idea that we each do our fair share to advance our common ends. But a system based on reciprocity is always vulnerable to the threat of *free-riding*, which occurs when people consume the benefits of cooperative action without doing any of the work that makes those benefits possible. The problem with unconditional benefits like a UBI is that they seem to encourage free-riding. That's not only a recipe for economic inefficiency; it's also, according to this way of thinking, deeply unjust.

Advocates of a UBI have responded to this concern in a few different ways.[2] The first response is to note that the objection might be based on an unfounded worry. The assumption seems to be that a significant number of people are going to stop working and live entirely off the UBI. But how likely is that? Previous empirical studies of the UBI (see chapters 32–36) have not demonstrated any such effect. And despite the limits of those studies (see chapter 37), there is good reason to think that a UBI would not lead to large numbers of people leaving the workforce altogether, especially if the size of the UBI is modest (see chapter 49).

Second, advocates of UBI have pointed out a certain irony in the objection: their worries about the importance of work and "doing one's fair share" only ever seem to be applied to the poor. But what about the idle rich? The economist John Kenneth Galbraith noted the hypocrisy in saying that "Leisure is very good for the rich, quite good for Harvard professors—and very bad for the poor. The wealthier you are, the more you are thought to be entitled to leisure. For anyone on welfare, leisure is a bad thing."[3]

The third response grants the importance of reciprocity, and of minimizing free-riding, but denies that this undermines the case for an unconditional cash transfer of the sort involved in a UBI. Suppose we admit that everybody ought to make a positive contribution to society in some way, as a condition of their being eligible to receive the benefits of that society. It simply does not follow that this contribution needs to take the form of *work*, at least not if we understand "work" to mean "participation in the paid labor market." Parents who stay home to raise their children are making a positive contribution to society, but they are not "working" in this narrow sense of the term. The same is true of full-time volunteers, or artists, or community activists. In other words, we can't identify "making a positive contribution to society" with "working for a paycheck." And, therefore, even if a UBI *does* enable some people to live without working for a paycheck, this doesn't necessarily mean they aren't doing their fair share.

51

WON'T PEOPLE JUST
WASTE CASH?

In addition to unconditionality, another defining feature of a UBI is that it is in cash, no strings attached. To UBI supporters, this is one of its greatest virtues. Providing cash allows people to decide what best meets their needs, recognizes that we all deserve autonomy and dignity, and is more efficient than in-kind transfers. But to detractors, this is one of its greatest vices. Isn't it obvious that poor people will just waste a UBI on drugs, alcohol, gambling, or other expenditures that are frivolous at best and harmful at worst?

In a word, no. The evidence actually suggests just the opposite—the vast majority of people who receive cash benefits do not waste them. Let's start with what we've seen during some UBI experiments and similar cash transfer programs in the developing world.[1] First, beneficiaries often spend their money in productive ways. Some make capital investments such as replacing a thatched roof with a metal roof or purchasing livestock. In Zambia, for example, cash transfers almost quintupled the number of households that owned goats; in Kenya, they increased livestock holdings by over 50%.[2] And many families increase spending on education, medical care, and food—especially vitamin and protein-rich foods such as meat, fruit, and vegetables.

Second, evidence suggests that beneficiaries do not increase—and in fact, sometimes decrease—spending on goods such as alcohol, cigarettes, drugs, or gambling. A fairly recent World Bank paper looked at nineteen studies on the relationship between cash transfers and spending on alcohol and tobacco; it concluded that "[a]lmost without exception, studies find either no significant impact or a significant negative impact of transfers on temptation goods."[3]

Additionally, measurable outcomes from these countries suggest beneficiaries are not frittering away cash transfers. A pre-pandemic study of GiveDirectly's program in Kenya, for example, suggested that the cash transfers increased food consumption by 19%. This in turn cut how many days children went without food by 42%, reduced the chance of going to bed hungry by 30%, and increased the chance of having enough food in the household for the next day by 20%. Another study of the same program during the pandemic showed an association between the transfers and improved well-being using measures such as hunger, sickness, and depression.[4] Other pre-pandemic studies echo these findings.[5] In Namibia, researchers found significant decreases in poverty and child malnutrition. And in India, an experimental UBI was found to have a positive correlation with health, school attendance, and school performance, as well as an association with reduced child labor.

People in the developed world, of course, aren't going to purchase goats and metal roofs. But as we've detailed elsewhere (see chapters 32–35), numerous studies from similar cash and cash-like transfer programs have found links between larger incomes and a variety of measures of well-being, suggesting that beneficiaries generally make productive use of such funds.

For example, associations have been found between the EITC and the Canada Child Benefit and higher math and reading scores, increased high school and college graduation rates, an enhanced chance of being employed in young adulthood, and measures of maternal and infant health such as increases in birth-weight and decreases in preterm birth.[6] Connections have also been found between receiving various governmental benefits when young and later having a lower chance of incarceration and a higher income.

Studies of non-governmental cash transfer programs mirror these results. One study of the Eastern Cherokee casino payments found that children in households receiving the payments stayed in school longer than those not receiving them; the $4,000 annual transfer to each household correlated with one additional year of schooling for each child. The same study also found a lower incidence of criminal behavior among children in families receiving transfers.[7]

These studies suggest that giving cash to families measurably improves their welfare.[8] If most people were frittering away cash transfers on drugs and alcohol, it is hard to imagine that we'd be seeing these types of improvements in well-being. So, although some people will unfortunately waste their benefits on vices like alcohol and drugs, most evidence suggests that this will be a very tiny minority.

52

WHAT ABOUT THE CHILDREN OF NEGLIGENT, MENTALLY ILL, DRUG-ADDICTED, OR ALCOHOLIC PARENTS?

A related fear is that unfit parents will waste a child's UBI instead of spending it to benefit that child, resulting in malnourished, poorly clothed children who live in squalor.[1] Instead of buying food or paying rent, some fear these parents will spend a child's UBI on drugs or alcohol or otherwise fritter it away. In theory, the in-kind provision of some necessities mitigates this risk—you can't trade a subsidized apartment for drugs.

It is unlikely, however, that such children will be worse off under a UBI. And in fact, some may even be better off, given that many current programs effectively exclude such families. First, many mentally ill or drug-addicted parents are unable to navigate the cumbersome application process required for many programs. Second, if such individuals are so unfit that they cannot hold a job, they do not benefit from programs such as the EITC that require work. Third, many existing welfare programs contain conditions that essentially prevent drug users from participating.[2] Consider TANF, which is the closest equivalent to cash welfare. Almost half the US states require beneficiaries who have past drug convictions or who trigger "reasonable suspicion" of drug abuse to submit to drug tests. Over two-thirds of the states ban convicted drug felons from TANF participation for some period of time—ten of them permanently.

Because of these hurdles to participation, many children in less-than-optimal family situations do not currently benefit from existing programs. We acknowledge that *some* unfit parents might well waste their child's UBI on drugs and alcohol (even if evidence shows that, on the whole, recipients do not use cash transfers to increase spending on drugs and alcohol, as we discuss in chapter 51).

But not all mentally ill or addicted parents will do so. It is quite likely that many such parents will spend at least part of their child's UBI on their child. Something is better than nothing, and it is hard to see how a UBI would render such children worse off than they currently are. Moreover, a parent's own UBI might enable him or her to seek treatment and create a more stable home environment. Again, not all parents will take advantage of such opportunities, but some might.

And lastly, implementing a UBI would not affect the current legal system that protects children from abuse and neglect, albeit imperfectly. Safeguards will still exist that enable a neglected or abused child to be removed from truly unsafe conditions.

53

COULD A BASIC INCOME MAKE THE POOR WORSE OFF?

What about the risk that a UBI might make the poor worse off? As we've seen, a UBI is a radical re-imagining of our social welfare scheme, and all policy changes have winners and losers. Some UBI opponents would have you believe that middle- and upper-income people would come out ahead if a UBI were implemented, and that the poor would be the losers. They argue that a UBI *necessarily* makes the poor worse off by funneling funds that would otherwise go to them into a UBI that people of all income levels receive. And it is true that if all benefit programs were eliminated and those funds were split among rich and poor alike, without imposing any new taxes, the poor would be worse off.

But as we've explained elsewhere (see chapters 8 and 9 especially), that's not how a UBI would actually work. Determining whether a UBI would make the poor worse off is more complicated than that. To start with, it would be almost impossible to implement a UBI in a way that doesn't leave someone, somewhere, worse off. This, of course, would be true of any new social policy. The question for UBI advocates is how to design such a UBI in a way that leaves as many people as possible better off, and as few people worse off, without breaking the bank.

At first, you might think that the easiest way to make sure nobody is worse off is to just add a UBI on top of existing programs, regardless of the cost (that is, implement a UBI-plus). Setting aside the question of whether tax *cuts* "trickle down" to the poor, it is quite plausible that the massive tax *increases* needed to finance a substantial UBI for all without replacing any existing programs would have some negative distortionary effects on the economy that would create spillover harm to the poor. So at the outset, it is unclear whether simply layering a UBI on top of other programs could even avoid this conundrum.

And as we've discussed in chapters 11 and 12, any UBI of more-than-minimal size would almost certainly be financed in part by rolling existing cash and near-cash transfer programs into a UBI (that is, be a UBI-minus). The size of the UBI, who will receive it, and what programs it will replace will determine how many people are helped and how many are harmed by its implementation.

For example, in the United States, implementing a UBI that eliminated Medicare, Medicaid, and CHIP (which provide health insurance to seniors and low-income individuals) and then required people to purchase their own health insurance with part of their UBI would almost certainly leave many, many poor people worse off. For that reason, most UBI plans would leave such programs intact; Charles Murray's is the notable exception.

Another US program whose elimination would appear to leave some families worse off—at least on paper—is Section 8, which provides housing vouchers. That said, very few eligible families actually participate in the program due to years-long waitlists. In San Diego, California, for example, the wait time for a voucher can be ten years![1] Moreover, many landlords refuse to take Section 8 vouchers; presumably they'd be unable to refuse to accept cash from a UBI. Given the small numbers of people actually helped by Section 8, eliminating it to help fund a UBI that would benefit many, many more people likely strikes most people as an acceptable trade off. And indeed, most UBI proposals in the United States appear to eliminate Section 8.

Who receives a UBI will also determine how many poor people will be worse off. Here, the treatment of children and seniors is crucial. At least in the United States, many existing programs heavily favor people with children. It's therefore highly unlikely that a UBI would leave many childless working-age adults worse off, but the same is not necessarily true for the very young and the very old.

Consider, for example, the effect of a $500 per-person per-month UBI on a two-parent two-child family of four.[2] Currently, that family might well be receiving SNAP (up to $835 per month for a family of four as of 2022);[3] the EITC (the equivalent of up to $498.33 per month); the Child Tax Credit (the equivalent of up to $600 per month for two children under the age of 6); and perhaps WIC (average monthly benefit of $35.44 per person). A UBI that included the children would yield this family $2,000 per month, which would offset the elimination of these programs. But a $500-per-month UBI that excluded children would leave this family far worse off.

You might think the issue disappears if the UBI were larger. And it is true that a $1,000 per-month per-adult UBI would also provide the family described above with $2,000 per month in aid. But that doesn't help single parents. A single mother with two children qualifies for the same potential EITC, CTC, and WIC benefits as the family above, but only a maximum of $658 per month in SNAP benefits. Assuming—and this is a big assumption, as we'll see—that she receives the maximum benefit, she is roughly $800 per month worse off under a $1,000-per-month UBI paid only to adults, but only roughly $300 per month worse off under a $500-per-month UBI that includes children.

What makes these comparisons tricky is that not that many people actually qualify for the maximum benefits. If our hypothetical single mother does not meet SNAP's work requirements, then she doesn't receive a dime from SNAP, although she'd receive a UBI. Likewise, if she is below the phase-in or over the phase-out threshold for earnings, she won't receive the full EITC. And as we've discussed elsewhere, the time and hassle it takes to sign up for existing welfare benefits is substantial, leading to less-than-ideal take up rates. For example, nationally, only about 80% of eligible beneficiaries enroll in SNAP, compared to what could easily be a UBI take up rate of almost 100%. So it's hard to know for sure how many mothers fitting the profile above would actually be worse off.

It's easier to see that a UBI that replaced Social Security, especially if it excluded seniors, would leave some seniors worse off. As of January 2022, the average monthly Social Security payment for retirees was $1,614 per month.[4] Replacing those benefits with a $1,000-per-month UBI, let alone a $500-per-month UBI, would leave millions of seniors worse off. This would be compounded if other programs that low-income seniors rely on, like SNAP, were also eliminated.

To minimize the number of people who would be worse off under a UBI, some advocates have proposed allowing people to choose. Murray, for example, suggests allowing seniors to choose between Social Security benefits and a UBI; Yang suggests allowing everyone to choose between their existing benefits and a UBI.

54

WILL A BASIC INCOME INCREASE HOSTILITY TO IMMIGRANTS?

Another concern is whether a UBI would increase hostility to immigrants. If it excludes non-citizens—as most major UBI proposals in the States do—then a UBI shouldn't affect attitudes toward immigration.

But if a polity decided to extend a UBI to all newcomers right away, regardless of immigration status, there are several reasons doing so might increase hostility to immigrants. Citizens might fear it would increase illegal immigration or encourage people to overstay visas, or make immigration more attractive to lower-skilled or less-motivated individuals. And, of course, immediately paying a UBI to new entrants would make a UBI more expensive. This would increase hostility not only to new immigrants, but potentially also to the idea of a UBI itself.

These concerns are present, however, with respect to any social benefit scheme. In theory, a UBI should only increase hostility if its requirements were looser—or if they were perceived to be looser—than those of existing cash and near-cash programs. As discussed in chapter 16, most such programs in the United States already restrict access to newcomers somehow. For example, SNAP and SSI have length-of-residency requirements, and the EITC by definition requires earned income. A compromise solution, such as imposing a waiting period or extending a UBI only to lawful permanent residents, could thus minimize potential hostility to immigrants. In particular, the latter should allay the fears about illegal entry or overstaying a visa, as well as concerns about unskilled entrants changing the mix of new arrivals.

55

WILL A BASIC INCOME CAUSE INFLATION?

Whether a UBI will cause inflation is a common fear. If everyone suddenly has several thousand more dollars per year to spend, won't prices just rise accordingly? The fear of rampant inflation is probably overblown, although prices might rise somewhat. However, a lot depends on how you pay for a UBI and certain location-specific factors.

First, a UBI that was solely a replacement for existing cash and cash transfer programs shouldn't affect inflation much, if at all, as it would not increase the overall supply of money even in a given locality. It simply changes the way existing benefit dollars are labeled and packaged, how often they are distributed, and who sends them out. Instead of a state agency giving a new mother paper WIC coupons, cash would be deposited into an account or onto a debit card. But the mother will probably purchase roughly the same amount of milk, or perhaps a bit more milk and a bit less of something else or vice versa. Instead of the IRS giving a working-class family a large tax refund once a year, the UBI agency gives that family its benefits monthly or bi-weekly. But the family won't actually have more money than before the switch from a tax credit to a UBI—they'll still only be able to afford one new appliance, not two. Even if some individuals receive larger benefits than before, others may receive fewer benefits. But the overall amount of transfer payments won't change much, which should render inflation concerns moot.

In fact, one can envision scenarios where prices for certain goods might decrease. In the United States, for example, parents can buy food but not diapers or vitamins with their SNAP benefits, and WIC specifies which types of food—white eggs but not brown, for example—and sometimes even which brands a new mother may buy! Moreover, mental accounting creates what economists call the "flypaper effect."[1] Imagine that *Ava*, who spends $200 per month on food and $400 per month on other necessities, begins receiving $100 worth of food stamps. The flypaper effect suggests that she is more likely to increase her spending on food more than on her other needs, even though she theoretically could continue spending $200 per month on food (via a mix of food stamps and cash) and increase her other spending by the newly freed up $100 cash.

Even with these limits and incentives, most evidence suggests that SNAP benefits increase prices only negligibly, if at all. A UBI that replaces SNAP and similarly targeted programs with cash would necessarily allow consumers to spend their dollars on a larger array of goods. Whether this increased competition for these consumer dollars will lower prices is an open question, but it is plausible to assume that at minimum it will not increase prices more than the current system.[2]

That's a UBI that doesn't increase the overall amount of governmental transfers. But even a UBI that does increase the overall amount of assistance paid out, as most proposals would, shouldn't create economy-wide inflation if financed by new taxes. Although individuals at the low end of the spectrum would have more cash to spend than before, those at the higher end would have less. It is likely that these would largely offset each other, especially in more developed countries with integrated economies and in which lower-income individuals are not geographically isolated.

This follows because of how markets work. You might wonder, for example, why landlords won't simply increase rent by $500 per month if a $500 UBI were instituted. Imagine that *Gary* tries to do just that, increasing rent on an apartment he owns from $1,000 to $1,500. If *Hannah* can rent out a similar unit for less than $1,500 per month, say $1,400, she'll lure tenants away from *Gary*. And if *Ivan* can undercut *Hannah*, he'll steal tenants from her. As before the UBI, market competition will limit the extent to which producers can raise prices.

Some evidence from existing cash transfer programs buttresses our intuition that fears of rampant inflation are overblown. First, a recent systematic review found that randomized control trials of such programs in developing countries generally had little to no impact on price. The exceptions tend to occur in isolated communities with few merchants and producers such that the increased funds are "trapped" or if other factors create monopolistic or oligarchic circumstances. In such contexts, prices may rise somewhat. Studies of cash and in-kind transfers in Mexico, for example, suggest that cash transfers increased food prices modestly (by about 1.5%) in less developed, remote villages, although they did not have a significant effect in most communities. Evidence from cash transfer programs in the Philippines and in Indonesia echo these findings in similar circumstances.[3]

Evidence from developed countries is not particularly conclusive, but generally suggests that any UBI-induced inflation would likely be small. The few studies finding that SNAP benefits increase prices aren't necessarily comparable to UBI payments, due to SNAP's restrictions and the flypaper effect just discussed. A recent study of the Alaska Permanent Fund by economists from the University of Chicago and the University of Pennsylvania found a small but not "statistically significant effect on prices or inflation" that the authors described as "extremely imprecise."[4] They further noted that this finding does not cause them to reevaluate their prior beliefs that large-scale cash transfer payments might have "small inflationary effects," but they emphasize that much uncertainty remains. What is telling for our purposes is that the paper focuses on "small" inflationary effects, implicitly ruling out large ones.

Lastly, these conclusions might seem surprising, given the recent confluence of sizable cash stimulus checks in many countries during the Covid-19 pandemic and the highest inflation levels in decades.[5] Two points. First, the Covid-19 payments were largely financed through deficit spending (that is, by borrowing instead of by higher taxes), and much agreement exists that inflation is most likely to be a problem if a UBI is financed by printing money or deficit spending. In these situations, a UBI increases the cash supply instead of simply rearranging it, triggering inflation.[6] Second, multiple additional factors also contributed to the high inflation rates, such as pent-up demand, supply issues, and labor shortages.[7] The unique circumstances of the Covid-19 relief payments are therefore not particularly illustrative when it comes to inflation and a UBI.

56

WHAT HAPPENS IF SOMEONE WASTES THEIR BASIC INCOME AND IS STILL HUNGRY AND HOMELESS?

Another common objection is that some people will waste their UBI and still be hungry and homeless. And unfortunately, this will almost certainly be the case. A UBI does not guarantee that nobody will ever find themselves in dire straits. This is true even if a UBI supplemented existing welfare programs instead of replacing them. In that case, someone who wastes their UBI would be in exactly the same position as they are now—either they take advantage of traditional aid programs, or they don't. But it's hard to see how adding a UBI to their options harms such individuals.

But if a UBI has replaced in-kind programs that would normally feed and house such individuals, what is to be done? Presumably, the same thing that happens now to people who don't take advantage of existing benefits. Despite current welfare programs, some people still go hungry and are unhoused. They might have past drug or other convictions that bar them from current aid programs, or they are unable to keep a job. Perhaps they have mental conditions that make it hard for them to fill out the required forms and keep the required appointments, or to comply with rules for governmental housing aid. These are likely the very people whom we fear would waste a UBI and still find themselves destitute.

Currently, some of those individuals turn to private programs, such as charity-run shelters and soup kitchens, or to friends and family. And those fallbacks would still exist. A UBI precludes neither charities nor friends and family from helping. Unfortunately, some people can't—or won't—avail themselves of this type of help either. For these people, providing aid in the form of a UBI doesn't really change anything.

That said, providing cash with no strings attached might actually help some individuals who are unable to comply with the type of restrictions commonly imposed by, for example, homeless shelters. Even if such individuals waste much of their UBI, they might potentially be better off than under the current system if they spend even a fraction of their UBI on food.

In short, no form of aid eliminates hunger and homelessness. A UBI, regardless of generosity, is no different. There will, unfortunately, always be individuals who find themselves on the margins. Some particularly challenged individuals will be harmed by a UBI's unconditional nature. Imagine, for example, someone who can convince existing welfare officers they deserve the current array of in-kind aid and who takes advantage of that aid, but is unable to navigate finding food and shelter on her own, as would be required by a UBI that replaced such programs. Our hunch is that such individuals are few and far between. Moreover, others will be helped by a UBI's unconditionality, such as those who have trouble jumping through the hoops of the existing welfare bureaucracy but could find food and shelter on their own if benefits were more accessible.

57

WHAT WOULD STOP A BASIC INCOME FROM GETTING BIGGER AND BIGGER OVER TIME?

Lastly, we've seen that one of the main objections to a UBI is that it would be too expensive (see chapter 48). In response to this objection, proponents of a UBI have sought to design various proposals that would be relatively affordable. But even if their numbers check out, there still remains a daunting problem: what's to stop the UBI from getting bigger, and less affordable, after it has been implemented?[1]

This worry is not based in idle speculation. If we look to experience, it turns out that most government social welfare programs have grown substantially over time. In 1940, Social Security constituted just 0.29% of all Federal expenditures. By 1960 that number had grown to 12.58%. By 2000 it was 22.88%.[2] Similarly, Medicare went from 3% of Federal spending in 1970 to 12% in 2020.[3]

Why does this happen? In the case of Medicare, the rising costs of medical treatment no doubt play a significant role. But there is a deeper and more general explanation as well. Every new government transfer program creates a constituency with a vested interest in the maintenance and expansion of that program. The reason that Social Security is regarded as the "third rail" of American politics is that any politician who proposes to reduce benefits will face the overwhelming wrath of voters who benefit from that program. And those same voters will generously reward those politicians who propose to increase spending on their favored program.

Of course, there are numerous other citizens who pay more than they benefit from Social Security. But for reasons first identified by the political scientist Mancur Olson, small concentrated interest groups tend to have an easier time coordinating to advance their interests than do larger, more dispersed groups.[4] When the costs of a program are dispersed widely over the entire taxpaying population, and the benefits concentrated narrowly upon a much smaller subset of that population, the latter group will be motivated to invest substantially more time, money, and effort in fighting to expand the program than the former will to contract it.

Of course, whether the growth of a UBI is a good thing or a bad thing depends on your perspective. Some advocates who favor a relatively generous UBI nevertheless recommend starting with something smaller as a first step. The idea is that political opposition to a "partial basic income" would be easier to overcome, and once in place, the program could be progressively expanded over time.[5]

As for those who see the potential growth of a UBI as a problem, there are two responses available. The first is that the problem is one that applies to *all* transfer programs, not just the UBI. So, if the proposal is to "swap out" certain existing programs in exchange for a UBI, it's not at all obvious that the problem would get any *worse* as a result. There's nothing special about a UBI that makes it especially prone to creeping expansion.

But perhaps more than this can be said. According to a second response, the UBI is actually *less* prone to this sort of expansion than other welfare programs. Why? Precisely because the program is *universal*, it does not create a distinct narrow interest group with interests opposed to the population as a whole. Transfer programs that are based on general rules that do not discriminate between different groups of people are, as the public choice economist James Buchanan has argued, less prone to rent-seeking and manipulation.[6] Moreover, because the UBI is a relatively *simple* and *transparent* policy, it is easier for the public to keep tabs on its size and cost than it is for more complicated programs like Social Security, Medicaid, or food stamps.

Neither of these responses guarantees that a UBI will not expand over time. But they do suggest that *in comparison with the present system*, we have no more reason to worry about a UBI, and quite possibly we have even less.

Part 7

THE POLITICS OF A UBI

58

IS A BASIC INCOME POLITICALLY FEASIBLE?

If you've read this far, chances are that the idea of a UBI has captured your imagination in some way. And you might also be wondering if the concept has any chance at all of being implemented, or if this is simply yet another idea that seems interesting on paper but whose time will never come.

As Yogi Berra quipped, it's tough to make predictions, especially about the future. But according to some recent surveys, the idea of a UBI has grown increasingly popular among Americans. Two polls conducted in 2021 showed that a majority of Americans support some form of UBI (55% in one poll, 67% in the other).[1] An earlier poll back in 2011 found that only 11% of Americans supported a UBI at the time. So, interest in the UBI seems to be blossoming among the American public. Could this mean that a UBI has a reasonable chance of being implemented in the near future?

Maybe. But we should be wary of concluding too much on the basis of polls like these. The problem with polls is that the questions they ask are always short on details. But as we have seen, when it comes to the UBI, the details matter—*a lot*.

Polls ask respondents whether they support a universal basic income. But in a way, that's a meaningless question. As we discussed in chapter 1, there is no single, identifiable policy called a "universal basic income." What that phrase really refers to is a *family* of loosely related policies, all of which involve cash transfers. But there is considerable variance among those policies, not only in how "universal" and "basic" they are, but along a host of other dimensions as well. Should the transfer be paid to individuals or to families?

To individuals with high earned income, or only to those whose income falls below a certain threshold? To children, or only adults? And how *much* cash should be transferred? Should it vary according to geography and cost of living? And how exactly are we going to pay for all this?

But the real problem isn't just that the idea of a UBI is unclear. The real problem is that this lack of clarity leads to the *appearance* of agreement where deep conflict really exists. Conservatives like Charles Murray and progressives like Philippe Van Parijs might both say they want a UBI. But that term means something very different to the two of them. Murray envisions a UBI as a modest benefit funded by dismantling almost all of the current welfare state. Van Parijs envisions a substantially larger benefit added on *top* of most currently existing programs. Murray's UBI would almost certainly be completely unacceptable to Van Parijs, and vice versa.

What this means is that there is probably less consensus about the desirability of a UBI than there appears to be. However, much the same could be said about a number of big policy goals, from climate change mitigation to health care reform. Any major political change is likely going to require compromise between groups with very different interests and ideologies. So where does that leave us?

One strategy for advancing a UBI's political prospects is to push for policy changes that move in the *direction* of a UBI, without adopting a UBI wholesale. So, for instance, consolidating some current in-kind transfer programs into a single cash grant would move the welfare state *closer* to what advocates of a UBI envision. Similarly, the recent (yet temporary) changes to the Child Tax Credit made that policy into something like a "UBI for children" (see chapter 28). Not quite universal, but still a kind of basic cash income.

Assistance for children is politically more popular among Americans than assistance for able-bodied adults. Similarly, conditional transfer programs tend to be more popular than unconditional ones. So, adopting conditional, cash transfer programs that target families might be a more effective way of getting a large-scale permanent system of cash transfers up and running. Whether that eases the way to a more universal or unconditional UBI, or makes it more difficult by "buying off" key constituencies is a difficult question of political strategy.

What seems clear, though, is that interest in the UBI is at a higher level now than at almost any point in the nation's—and the world's—history. It has probably never had a better chance of becoming policy than it does today—even if that chance remains small, all-things-considered. This final portion of the book will therefore explore the UBI through various political lenses, in order to get a better handle on the question of how politically feasible a UBI actually is.

59

IS THE BASIC INCOME A SOCIALIST IDEA?

There is a tendency in the United States to describe any large government social welfare program as "socialist." The New Deal was criticized as socialist in the 1930s, and the Affordable Care Act was criticized as socialist in the 2000s. Those who see things in this way are likely to decry the UBI as socialist as well.

But a UBI certainly isn't socialist in the *strict* sense of the term. Strictly speaking, a socialist is someone who believes that private property in the "means of production" ought to be abolished, and replaced with ownership by the public, or the government. Under a purely socialist regime, factories, banks, restaurants, airlines, etc. would no longer by owned and operated by profit-seeking capitalists, but would instead be administered by the government for the benefit of the public at large. The role of markets in economic organization would be significantly curtailed, if not abolished altogether, replaced by some form or another of centralized economic planning.

Nothing in the idea of a UBI requires any of *that*. You can have a UBI without abandoning capitalism. In fact, arguably the whole point of a UBI is to make life easier for people to get by in the context of a capitalist system. After all, if things like food and housing were provided for free by the state rather than sold in capitalist markets, what would be the point of giving people money?

So, there is nothing in the logic of a UBI that entails socialism. But what about the reverse? Does anything in the logic of socialism entail a UBI?

The answer to this question is also "no"; strictly speaking, socialism doesn't *require* a UBI. There is, however, an interesting debate regarding whether socialism is *compatible* with a UBI, or whether certain socialist ideas might even *support* a UBI, without strictly speaking requiring it.

For example, one socialist theorist has argued that a UBI would help to advance three important socialist goals: 1) strengthening the power of labor vis-à-vis capital, 2) decommodifying labor by freeing individuals from the compulsion of entering the labor market, and 3) enlarging the potential for a social economy by making it easier for people to form workers' cooperatives and other forms of collective economic provision.[1] On this view, a UBI is not exactly a *socialist* policy. But it is a policy that could move capitalism in the *direction* of socialism.

However, not all socialists support a UBI. At a minimum, socialists would want to ensure that the kind of UBI adopted would not leave the poor worse off than they are under the present system (see chapter 53). Most socialists suspect that proposals that would fund a UBI by eliminating most other welfare programs would do just this.

Beyond that, however, some socialists see the whole idea of a UBI as fundamentally the wrong approach to social reform.[2] After all, for socialists the problem is *capitalism* as such, not merely the poverty and inequality that happen to go along with it. If a UBI would help to make capitalism work better—if it would help ease the suffering of the poor and thereby reduce popular dissatisfaction with capitalism—that is a drawback, not an advantage. On this view, a UBI merely helps to prop up a structure that is fundamentally unsound, and thereby serves only to delay the needed radical reform.

60

WHAT DO CONSERVATIVES THINK ABOUT A BASIC INCOME?

That's socialism. What about conservatism? American conservatism is notoriously difficult to define, in large part because it has evolved out of a mix of distinct and sometimes conflicting ideological elements. There is a strand of traditionalism based on the kinds of ideas expressed in the writing of Edmund Burke, which counsels respect for established practices and institutions, and skepticism toward sweeping, radical change. There is a religious strand that stresses obedience to God and the development of moral virtue. There is a communitarian element that focuses on the role of families and communities in a good society. And there is a libertarian element that emphasizes free markets and limited government.

The most significant conservative defense of a UBI is Charles Murray's *In Our Hands: A Plan to Replace the Welfare State*. Depending on which aspects of his thought you choose to focus on, Murray is either a libertarian-leaning conservative, or a conservative-leaning libertarian. For clarity, we will focus on the libertarian elements of Murray's argument elsewhere (see chapter 63). Here, we focus on those aspects of his argument that are distinctly conservative in nature.

Individual Responsibility

One of the moral virtues on which conservatives place a great deal of emphasis is individual responsibility. Conservatives believe that people must bear the consequences of their actions, whether good or bad. In part they believe this because the only alternative is for someone *else* to bear the consequences, which seems unfair. And in part they believe it because it is the most effective way of teaching people to make better decisions over time. If bad choices don't lead to bad consequences, then why bother learning how to make good choices instead?

One of the advantages of a UBI, from this perspective, is that it encourages this sort of responsibility. Because a UBI takes the form of an unrestricted cash grant, people must decide for themselves what to do with the money, and bear the consequences. A UBI is not paternalistic. It does not try to steer people toward any pre-conceived notion of the good life. A UBI gives people freedom, as well as the responsibility that goes along with that freedom.

Families and Communities

Conservatives recognize, however, that human beings are not atomistic, self-sufficient individuals. Human beings live in and depend on larger groups such as families and communities for their survival and well-being. Siblings lend each other money or a place to stay during hard times, neighbors bring food and emotional support, churches provide counseling, community, and other forms of material assistance.

Because Murray's UBI would *replace* many social welfare programs that are currently administered by the state, he believes that it would provide an opening for families and communities to step up and reclaim the functions that had been "crowded out" by government growth. A UBI might also strengthen families by removing the disincentives to marriage inherent in the existing welfare system. See chapters 44 and 45 for further discussion.

Conservative Objections to a UBI

Needless to say, not all conservatives support a UBI. Some conservatives object on fiscal grounds—a UBI, they believe, would be too expensive and would require either higher taxes (which would stifle the economy), or higher deficits (which would unfairly burden future generations). Many conservatives also worry that a

UBI would disincentivize work, which might create a further drag on the economy.[1]

But for many conservatives, the issue of work disincentives is not exclusively (or even primarily) an economic issue. For many, it is a *moral* issue. Work, for these conservatives, is not merely a means to acquiring an income. It is an exercise of virtue and individual responsibility, and an important component in a satisfying, meaningful life. To the extent that a UBI discourages people from working, it diminishes the quality of their lives, *even if their income remains unchanged.*

Similarly, the main objection that many conservatives have against the current welfare state is not the cost but the *dependency* they believe it creates. When the safety net becomes so comfortable that it serves as a permanent resting place rather than a temporary respite, people learn to rely on government rather than their own initiative for their comfort. If a UBI would make this problem worse, many conservatives will see that as a decisive reason to reject it.

61

WHAT HAVE FEMINISTS SAID ABOUT A BASIC INCOME?

What about feminist concerns? Would a UBI improve the position of women? Would it advance the cause of gender equality? Feminists have long been interested in the UBI as an instrument of social change. But not all feminists believe that adopting a UBI would represent a change for the better. This chapter briefly surveys some of the main feminist arguments for and against a UBI.

Compensating Unpaid Care

Traditionally, much of the work that women do has been unpaid. Women are much more likely than men to be acting as full-time caregivers, raising children, preparing meals, and doing household maintenance. And even when women do work outside the home, a disproportionate share of household work still falls on their shoulders.

Caregiving is valuable—indeed, *essential*—work. So why doesn't society compensate it? Our failure to do so arguably reflects the lack of value we place on such work, as compared with work outside the home. And that failure to properly value caregiving is itself likely rooted in sexist beliefs and attitudes. A UBI could help to rectify this problem by providing some recognition and compensation for the caregiving work that women do.

Improving the Position of Women

A UBI would help send the signal that society values the work that women do. But the money a UBI provides would also make a real, material difference in women's lives. Women who are full-time caregivers are entirely dependent upon their partner's paycheck for their financial needs. This dependency severely limits their ability to make autonomous, independent choices within the relationship. It also makes it difficult for them to *exit* the relationship, a fact which is especially worrisome in cases where the relationship is abusive and the husband exercises strict control over the money he earns outside the home.

By providing women with an independent, individual stream of income, a UBI can increase women's autonomy and increase their bargaining position within the home.

What about Gender Equality?

Some feminists, however, criticize the UBI for failing to address fundamental issues of gender inequality within society. Giving women caregivers money might make their lives easier, but it doesn't change the fact that women are doing most of the caregiving work while men are working outside the home. For these feminists, the traditional gendered division of labor is *itself* a problem, quite separate from the question of whether women are compensated for the work they do.[1] At the very least, then, the UBI will not *suffice* to produce gender equality. It would need to be part of a larger packet of social policy measures.

UBI vs the Welfare State

Still other feminists argue that the UBI is not only insufficient for achieving gender equality—but that it is fundamentally the wrong approach. Barbara Bergmann, for instance, notes that Swedish-style welfare states provide a number of services that are of special value to women—paid maternity leave, childcare, health care, and so on.[2] But such an expansive welfare state does not come cheaply. Sweden's welfare state consumes approximately 60% of its GDP. It would not be fiscally possible, then, to simply *add* a UBI on top of such a welfare state. And *replacing* part of the Swedish welfare state with a UBI would arguably make women worse off by channeling money away from programs that benefit women specifically and toward universal programs that spread benefits more thinly over the entire population. It is unlikely that a UBI would be large enough to adequately cover the difference—especially since the costs of childcare can easily amount to half a woman's yearly earnings or more.

62

WHAT DO PROGRESSIVES THINK ABOUT A BASIC INCOME?

Both in the United States and abroad, the majority of the political support for the UBI comes from the progressive left.[1] Even among progressives, however, the idea of a UBI is controversial. This chapter will explore some of the reasons progressives support a UBI, as well as some of their reservations.

Redistribution

A UBI can be designed in such a way as to be highly redistributive. For many on the left, this is the single most important attraction of a UBI. The poor have more urgent unmet needs than the wealthy— the need to buy food, to purchase basic medical care, to keep the lights on. Taking money from those who have plenty and giving it to those who don't have enough strikes many on the left as a basic matter of social justice.[2]

Of course, the distributive effects of a UBI depend almost entirely on the details of how it is designed. And so here, as elsewhere, progressive support for a UBI will depend on the particular *kind* of UBI under consideration. More on this below.

Income as a Right

A UBI is redistributive. But so are many donations to private charitable organizations. What makes the UBI different from charitable programs is that it establishes an income stream that the poor can claim as a matter of *right*. A UBI is not charity—it is an *entitlement*.

As a practical matter, this is important because it means the income is something that recipients can count on. The predictability of a UBI allows individuals to plan and budget around it, and this in turn helps to minimize the unnecessary expenses involved with last-minute and unplanned purchases (late fees, interest rates, etc.).

But even beyond these practical matters, establishing a UBI as a right also has a symbolic significance. It says something about the status and worth of the individual in our society, and our obligations as a society to each individual. It sends the message that people's ability to meet their basic needs is not something that should be left to the chance and contingency of the market, but rather an obligation that we collectively take upon ourselves to meet as a matter of justice.

Protecting the Vulnerable

Low-income families need money to meet their basic needs. But money does more than purchase goods and services. Money also provides the poor with the freedom to say "no."[3]

This fact matters because to be poor is to be in a position of tremendous vulnerability. The poor use a disproportionately large share of their income to meet their most basic human needs—food and shelter. Because these needs are non-optional, the poor must often take whatever opportunities they can to meet them. And so, if the only way to pay the rent or buy groceries is to work overtime, or pay the high interest for a payday loan, or to take $50 from the pawn broker for your mother's wedding ring, then the poor often have no choice but to say "yes."

A UBI gives the poor the power to say "no." By providing an alternative means for meeting their basic needs, a UBI provides some degree of protection from those who would unscrupulously seek to take advantage of their vulnerability. It means that the poor don't have to accept an offer *just because* it's the only offer on the table. It doesn't alleviate the problems of poverty altogether. But it does buy some room to breathe.

Progressive Objections to a UBI

The main objection that progressives have against a UBI is that—depending on how it is structured—it could leave the poor worse off than they are under the current system (see chapter 53).

This might happen if, as conservatives like Charles Murray would like, a UBI *replaces* sizeable portions of the existing welfare state. There are two potential problems with such an approach to implementing a UBI. The first is that, according to some analyses, it might make the poor financially worse off than they are under the current system.[4] Many existing programs are means-tested, and directed specifically toward the poor. The fear is that if those programs are replaced by a universal program that directs money toward everyone, then the poor will receive a smaller share of money than they do now. We've talked elsewhere about how a UBI most likely wouldn't really be universal, but it is true that most UBI proposals would benefit more people than the current system. So, depending on how a UBI is structured, it is true that the poor could receive a smaller share than they currently do.

The other way in which replacing the welfare state with a UBI might make the poor worse off is by swapping out *services* for *cash*. The argument for a UBI is based on the assumption that cash is always better than in-kind benefits, since people can use cash to buy whatever they value most. But there are some cases where this argument clearly doesn't work. You don't make an alcoholic better off by giving them cash rather than treatment. Similarly, it's not obvious that you make children better off by giving their parents cash instead of a free school lunch program. Sometimes, the problem is that we don't actually trust that individuals will use the money in the best way to advance their needs or the needs of their family. In other cases, the worry is that there are certain kinds of services—perhaps medical care—that because of economies of scale or other factors are better provided directly by the government than indirectly through the market.

Progressives want the government to do what it can to help the poor and vulnerable and are generally willing to endure significantly higher taxes in order to achieve this goal. For this group, then, the question that divides supporters of a UBI from detractors is: will a UBI make the poor better off, or worse?

63

WHAT DO LIBERTARIANS THINK ABOUT A BASIC INCOME?

If there is one group that seems more likely than others to vehemently oppose a UBI, it's libertarians. Libertarians, after all, believe in free markets and strictly limited government.[1] Many, like Murray Rothbard, believe that "taxation is theft," and therefore oppose *all* government-funded social welfare programs.[2] For people like this, a UBI that doles out large amounts of taxpayers' money indiscriminately would seem to be beyond the pale.

As we will see later in this chapter, many libertarians *do* in fact oppose a UBI. But, perhaps surprisingly, a number of fairly well-known libertarians have expressed support for a UBI, or something very close to it.[3] The libertarian economist Milton Friedman, for instance, was a vocal supporter of the Negative Income Tax (NIT—discussed in chapter 29). Though a libertarian, Friedman thought the government had a legitimate role to play in alleviating poverty in order to overcome certain collective action problems associated with purely private charity. But, he thought, if the government is going to try to relieve poverty, it should do so in the most efficient way possible. Minimum wage laws and price supports undermine efficiency by distorting the signals created by the price system. But a simple cash grant has only minimal distortive effects, and helps the poor in a way that is effective and transparent.[4]

Friedrich Hayek, author of *The Road to Serfdom* and numerous other works in social theory, also thought that society should provide "a certain amount of income for everyone . . . a sort of floor below which nobody need fall even when he is unable to provide for himself."[5] Hayek's proposal wasn't quite a *universal* basic income, however. According to Hayek, only those who were genuinely *incapable* of supporting themselves should be eligible for support. Those who were able to work but chose not to, Hayek thought, had no claim on the state for support (see chapter 50). Still, subject to this constraint, Hayek believed that the assurance of a "minimum income for everyone" was not only a "wholly legitimate protection against a common risk to all" but a necessary part of a large-scale market society where individuals cannot always rely on their family or community for support.

In addition to Friedman and Hayek's arguments, there are other, less well-known, libertarian arguments that have been made on behalf of a UBI. One of us has argued, for example, that a UBI might be justifiable on libertarian grounds as reparation for injustices committed by the state in the past.[6] A libertarian UBI might also be grounded in the so-called Lockean Proviso, a principle that places a constraint on the acquisition of property rights by individuals in order to protect the rightful claims of others.[7]

Other libertarians—sometimes referred to as "left-libertarians"—base their argument for a UBI on the idea that the Earth and all its resources are the common property of humanity.[8] These libertarians agree with John Locke that individuals are self-owners—that they own their bodies and their labor. But they disagree with "right-libertarians" about the implications of self-ownership for the ownership of external resources. After all, nobody *created* the land or the oil and minerals under it. And so, no individual has any justification for fencing those resources off and excluding everyone else from using them.

For some left-libertarians, the only reason to allow private property in natural resources is that doing so helps ensure that those resources will be used efficiently. But as the 20th-century economist and social reformer Henry George argued, we can allow individuals to *control* natural resources without also allowing them to *profit* from them.[9] If we allow individuals to keep what they create with their labor, but tax the full value of the unimproved natural resource itself (the so-called "Single Tax"), we can both respect individual self-ownership and reclaim for society the value that rightfully belongs to it. That value can then be redistributed to others, perhaps in the form of a UBI.[10]

Still, most libertarians remain skeptical of a UBI, at least when the UBI is funded by taxation rather than as a private philanthropic activity (see chapter 33). Many libertarians believe that *any* taxation for redistributive purposes is unjust.[11] For these libertarians, a UBI is unacceptable, but so too is any other form of social welfare program. Other, less stringent libertarians might accept that some form of limited or narrowly targeted redistribution is acceptable, but balk at the universality of a UBI. Morally, they might object to redistribution being used to give *everybody* money when only *some* people have a legitimate claim on it. And economically, they might worry that the *cost* of a universal benefit will be unreasonably high. This high cost will have to be paid for (eventually) with high taxes, which is both bad for the market and (for libertarians) objectionably coercive.

64

IS A BASIC INCOME LIKELY TO BE IMPLEMENTED ANYTIME SOON?

As we discussed in chapter 58, some opinion polls report a good deal of support among the public for a UBI. But we also pointed out that the results of these polls should be taken with a grain of salt. Even if the public agreed that a UBI is a good idea in *principle*, that's a long way from agreeing about which specific *kind* of UBI would be desirable.

And when it comes to implementing a UBI, public support is just the beginning of a long and difficult process. It's not enough for the public to be supportive of a UBI in an abstract, passive sort of way. That support needs to be effectively mobilized in order to make an impact on legislators. But this is harder than it sounds. As we discussed in chapter 57, smaller and more narrowly defined interest groups generally have an easier time organizing to advance their interests than broader, more dispersed ones. The very universality of a UBI might, therefore, actually be a strategic disadvantage when it comes to organizing for effective political action.

We can learn some valuable lessons about implementing a UBI by looking at the fate of Richard Nixon's Family Assistance Plan (FAP). This program, proposed by Nixon to a national audience in August 1969, is probably the closest any country has come to implementing a permanent, national UBI. At the time, there was tremendous public dissatisfaction with the existing welfare system, and a great deal of interest in the Negative Income Tax (NIT) as an alternative. Milton Friedman had popularized the idea in his 1962 book, *Capitalism and Freedom*.[1] And in 1968, over 1,000 economists signed a statement supporting a UBI.[2]

Despite these sources of support, however, Nixon's proposal failed. Even from the beginning, the idea fell short of a true UBI. The FAP would only cover families with children. And there was a work requirement of sorts—parents who were deemed able to work but who were unwilling to accept a job or job training would lose their benefits (but not their children's benefits). These deviations from the pure theory of a NIT were almost certainly a political necessity. The public would have been unwilling to support a policy that did not require recipients to work, and there was little interest in supporting adults without dependent children, let alone in paying the greatly increased cost such an expansion would create.

Watered down as it was, Nixon's proposal still couldn't attract the necessary support to make it through Congress. Conservatives worried that the FAP would be too expensive and would encourage dependency. Progressives complained that the program was too stringent and not generous enough. And interest groups surrounding already existing welfare programs mobilized against what they saw as a potential threat to their operations.

Finally, the numbers behind the program simply didn't add up. Friedman's idea of a NIT had involved *replacing* most existing welfare programs. On that assumption, he argued, an NIT would encourage work by removing many of the disincentives associated with the existing system (see chapter 49). But the FAP was to *supplement* existing welfare programs, not *substitute* them. As a result, while the FAP itself produced desirable incentives to work, its effect when combined with other programs was to produce shockingly high marginal effective tax rates on poorer workers. When working one more hour means losing a $1,000 housing benefit, no sane person will choose to work.[3] In the end, even Milton Friedman, the original architect of the Negative Income Tax, wrote that he could not support the idea as implemented in Nixon's FAP.[4]

What we can learn from Nixon's FAP is that implementing a UBI will be complicated. It will require substantive compromise between competing ideological groups, meaning that the resulting legislation will almost certainly differ substantially from any pure model envisioned by UBI advocates. It will require dealing with existing political and economic interest groups who may perceive their own welfare as threatened by a UBI. And it will require designing both expenses and finances in a way that makes the numbers work—not just in theory, but in the messy and generally unpredictable world of political budgets.

Of course, none of these considerations suggest that it is *impossible* to implement a UBI. Similar concerns could have been raised about the prospects of almost any major piece of social welfare legislation enacted in the United States over the past hundred years: from Social Security, to Medicare, to the Affordable Care Act.

Still, at the time of this writing there is no country in the world that is actively considering legislation to enact a UBI. There are a large number of pilot programs across the world, but so far there is little reason to believe that these pilots will translate into permanent, tax-funded programs. So, at this point, the prospects for implementing a permanent UBI anytime within the next several years seem slim.

65

ARE THERE ANY ORGANIZATIONS ADVOCATING FOR A BASIC INCOME?

There sure are. The oldest organization still in existence, Basic Income Earth Network, was launched almost forty years ago in Europe. Its purpose, like that of most of the other early organizations, was intellectual and abstract—to promote discussion and awareness of the idea of a UBI. More recently, however, several organizations with the explicit aim of turning these abstract ideas into political reality have launched. Here is a list of the major organizations advocating for a UBI, from oldest to newest.

- **Basic Income Earth Network** (www.basicincome.org)—Founded in 1986 as the Basic Income European Network, this organization changed its title in 2006 to reflect its more global reach and mission. The BIEN's mission is primarily educational rather than political in nature, and is focused on informing the public about "alternative arguments about, proposals for, and problems concerning, basic income as idea, institution, and public policy practice." BIEN hosts an annual conference, serves as a repository of research, and publishes news, research, and opinion pieces on the UBI.
- **The US Basic Income Guarantee Network** (www.usbig.net)— USBIG was launched in 1999. Like BIEN, it is an educational organization that runs an annual conference and publishes news, research, and opinion. Its focus, however, is limited to the United States.

- **Basic Income Canada Network** (www.basicincomecanada.org)— The main Canadian organization dedicated to promoting discussion of the UBI, founded in 2008.
- **GiveDirectly** (https://www.givedirectly.org/about/)—Give-Directly is not an advocacy organization per se, like the others we've included on this list. Instead, it has sponsored UBI pilot programs across the globe since 2009, focusing mainly on Africa, and published a large quantity of careful research based on those programs. Advocates often point to its experiences and its research. Donating to GiveDirectly is one way lay people can directly advance the cause of UBI, by putting their own dollars to work.
- **The Economic Security Project** (www.economicsecurityproject. org)—The ESP was started in 2016 to address problems of economic insecurity in the United States. It advocates for and funds research regarding the UBI, and also supports various anti-monopoly efforts aimed at reducing the concentration of economic power. The ESP was one of the major sponsors of the Stockton Economic Empowerment Demonstration, discussed in chapter 36.
- **Humanity Forward** (www.humanityforward.com)—Humanity Forward was started in 2020 by Andrew Yang. A national UBI was the central policy of Yang's campaign, and Humanity Forward carries that mission forward by working at the federal level to advance a range of policies involving direct cash transfers (such as the Child Tax Credit). It is one of the most directly political organizations on the list, with an active lobbying presence on Capitol Hill.
- **Mayors for a Guaranteed Income** (www.mayorsforagi.org)— Mayors for a Guaranteed Income was started in 2020 by the Economic Security Project and Michael Tubbs, then mayor of Stockton, California. It is a network of mayors advocating a UBI, and sponsoring pilot programs in various cities across the United States. At the time of this writing, more than forty such pilots are active.

66

WHERE CAN I LEARN MORE ABOUT A BASIC INCOME?

Today, there is a vast amount of information available for those hoping to learn more about a UBI. And with the growing body of academic research, the rapidly increasing pace of pilot programs, and increasing attention from major media outlets, more and more information is becoming available with each passing week. So much so that—take it from us!—it can be hard for even academic researchers focused on the topic to keep up.

So, if you're ready to dive in, here are a few sources to start learning more about a UBI. Needless to say, this is a very incomplete list! But once you start looking around, you should be able to find your way around and start exploring on your own within no time.

Books—Our hope is that this book has served you as a useful introduction to the UBI. But if you want to dive deeper, there are some other terrific books out there that can help you learn more about particular aspects of the UBI. *Basic Income: A Radical Proposal for a Free Society and a Sane Economy* by Philippe Van Parijs and Yannick Vanderborght is a scholarly and comprehensive treatment of the UBI by one of the earliest and most respected proponents of the idea. It covers the intellectual history of the idea, the philosophical arguments for and against, and the economic and political considerations relevant to implementing a basic income in today's world.[1] Evelyn Forget's *Basic Income for Canadians* is a useful overview of the UBI in a Canadian context, with a helpful discussion of Canada's MINCOME experiment and current policy prospects for the idea.[2] Karl Widerquist has authored several books on the UBI, including a guide to UBI experiments and a philosophical defense of UBI rooted in the value of freedom.[3] And *Debating Universal Basic Income: Pros, Cons, and Alternatives,* by Robert Wright and Aleksandra Przegalińska, provides an in-depth look at some of the most influential arguments both for and against a UBI.[4]

Geared toward a popular audience, Rutger Bregman, Guy Standing, and Annie Lowrey have all produced helpful and accessible treatments of UBI for a popular audience. And Chris Hughes, Andy Stern, Andrew Yang, and Charles Murray have all authored books that contain specific proposals, as well as overviews of many of the topics discussed in this book.[5]

Academic Journals—But if you're *really* looking to keep up with the latest academic research on the UBI, you'll want to check out *Basic Income Studies.* Founded in 2006, Basic Income Studies is the premier outlet for peer-reviewed research on the UBI. It publishes two issues per year, including the occasional special issue on topics such as "Basic Income and Employment in Developing Countries," "Should Feminists Endorse a UBI?," and "A Symposium on Basic Income Experiment Designs."

On the Internet—Books and journals are great for learning about the history, economics, and philosophy of the UBI. But if you want to know what's happening right now—and there's a lot of that!—you'll want to hit the internet. The Basic Income Earth Network hosts a website called Basic Income News that covers most major developments with the UBI, from new pilot programs to scholarly workshops to petition drives. Other helpful websites include that of Basic Income Today, the Basic Income Community on Reddit, and UBI advocate Scott Santens's site. Finally, check out Twitter! You can follow organizations such as BIEN (@BasicIncomeOrg), Basic Income Today (@UBIToday), and Basic Income (@BasicIncome), as well as Scott Santens (@ScottSantens).

NOTES

Chapter 2

1. Thomas Paine, "Agrarian Justice" (1797), in *The Origins of Universal Grants* (Basingstoke and New York: Springer, 2004), 3–16.
2. Henry George, *Progress and Poverty* (New York: D. Appleton and Company, 1886).
3. Peter Barnes, *With Liberty and Dividends for All: How to Save Our Middle Class When Jobs Don't Pay Enough* (San Francisco: Berrett-Koehler Publishers, 2014).
4. Thomas Spence, *The Rights of Infants; . . . in a Dialogue Between the Aristocracy and a Mother of Children. To Which Are Added, . . . Strictures on Paine's Agrarian Justice* (1797).
5. James E. Meade, *Agathotopia: The Economics of Partnership* (Aberdeen: Aberdeen University Press, 1989); Bertrand Russell, *Proposed Roads to Freedom: Socialism, Anarchism and Syndicalism* (New York: Holt, 1920).
6. Jyotsna Sreenivasan, ed., "A Statement by Economists on Income Guarantees and Supplements," in *Poverty and the Government in America* (Santa Barbara, CA: ABC-CLIO, 2009), 269. On the question of whether Hayek's proposal was really a UBI, see chapter 63.
7. Martin Luther King Jr., *Where Do We Go from Here: Chaos Or Community?* (Boston: Beacon Press, 1967).

Chapter 3

1. Andy Stern, *Raising the Floor: How a Universal Basic Income Can Renew Our Economy and Rebuild the American Dream* (New York: Public Affairs, 2016).
2. Charles A. Murray, *In Our Hands: A Plan to Replace the Welfare State*, 2nd ed. (Washington, D.C.: AEI Press, 2016).
3. Philippe Van Parijs and Yannick Vanderborght, *Basic Income: A Radical Proposal for a Free Society and a Sane Economy* (Boston: Harvard University Press, 2017).
4. See Karl Widerquist, *Independence, Propertylessness, and Basic Income: A Theory of Freedom as the Power to Say No* (New York: Palgrave Macmillan, 2013); Karl Widerquist, *A Critical Analysis of Basic Income Experiments for Researchers,*

Policymakers, and Citizens (New York: Springer, 2018); Karl Widerquist, "Reciprocity and the Guaranteed Income," *Politics and Society* 27, no. 3 (1999): 386–401.

5. Guy Standing, *Basic Income: And How We Can Make It Happen* (London: Pelican, 2017); Guy Standing, *Basic Income: A Guide for the Open-Minded* (New Haven, CT: Yale University Press, 2017); Annie Lowrey, *Give People Money: How a Universal Basic Income Would End Poverty, Revolutionize Work, and Remake the World* (New York: Crown, 2018); Evelyn L. Forget, *Basic Income for Canadians: From the COVID-19 Emergency to Financial Security for All* (Toronto: James Lorimer & Company, 2020); Rutger Bregman, *Utopia for Realists: How We Can Build the Ideal World* (New York: Little, Brown, 2018).

Chapter 4

1. Djavad Salehi-Isfahani and Mohammad H. Mostafavi-Dehzooei, "Cash Transfers and Labor Supply: Evidence from a Large-Scale Program in Iran," *Journal of Development Economics* 135 (2018): 349–67.
2. Randall K. Q. Akee, Willim E. Copeland, Gordon Keeler, Adrian Angold, and Jane E. Costello, "Parents' Incomes and Children's Outcomes: A Quasi-Experiment Using Transfer Payments from Casino Profits," *American Economic Journal: Applied Economics* 2, no. 1 (2010): 86–115.

Chapter 5

1. Andy Stern, *Raising the Floor: How a Universal Basic Income Can Renew Our Economy and Rebuild the American Dream* (New York: Public Affairs, 2016).
2. Charles Murray, *In Our Hands: A Plan to Replace the Welfare State*, 2nd ed. (Washington, D.C.: AEI Press, 2016).
3. See Karl Widerquist, *Independence, Propertylessness, and Basic Income: A Theory of Freedom as the Power to Say No* (New York: Palgrave Macmillan, 2013).
4. Philippe Van Parijs, *Real Freedom for All: What (If Anything) Can Justify Capitalism?*, Oxford Political Theory (New York: Oxford University Press, 1995). See also Widerquist, *Independence, Propertylessness, and Basic Income*.

Chapter 6

1. Robert Greenstein, "Commentary: Universal Basic Income May Sound Attractive But, If It Occurred, Would Likelier Increase Poverty Than Reduce It," *Center on Budget and Policy Priorities* (June 13, 2019), https://www.cbpp.org/research/poverty-and-opportunity/commentary-universal-basic-inc ome-may-sound-attractive-but-if-it.

Chapter 7

1. This chapter draws heavily from Miranda Perry Fleischer and Daniel Hemel, "The Architecture of a Basic Income," *The University of Chicago Law Review* 87 (2020): 665–71.
2. Although nothing requires a UBI to rise with inflation, we assume that it would be indexed to inflation and increase regularly—much like Social Security payments and traditional welfare benefits do.
3. Philippe Van Parijs and Yannick Vanderborght, *Basic Income: A Radical Proposal for a Free Society and a Sane Economy* (Boston: Harvard University Press, 2017).

4. Office of the Assistant Secretary for Planning and Evaluation, *HHS Poverty Guidelines for 2022* (January 12, 2022), archived at https://perma.cc/6LXZ-K8LU.

5. See Wankyo Chung, Hyungserk Ha, and Beomsoo Kim, "Money Transfer and Birth Weight: Evidence from the Alaska Permanent Fund Dividend," *Economic Inquiry* 54 (2016): 576, 581–3 (finding an 8–14 percent reduction in the incidence of low birth-weight—defined as less than or equal to 2.5 kg—infants as a result of the dividend).

6. US Department of Labor, Bureau of Labor Statistics, *The Employment Situation—May 2022* *tbl. B-8 (June 3, 2022), archived at https://perma.cc/AV48-C3GQ.

Chapter 8

1. Philippe Van Parijs and Yannick Vanderborght, *Basic Income: A Radical Proposal for a Free Society and a Sane Economy* (Boston: Harvard University Press, 2017), 8.

2. See Miranda Perry Fleischer and Daniel Hemel, "The Architecture of a Basic Income," *The University of Chicago Law Review* 87 (2020): 696.

3. Financing a UBI with a consumption tax such as a value-added tax (VAT) has a similar effect. Those who consume more, and therefore pay more under a consumption tax, would contribute more to the government than they receive. Although consumption does not increase as sharply as income (it is unlikely Jeff Bezos consumes 200,000 times as much as the authors), it certainly increases to some extent. Jeff Bezos consumes considerably more than the authors, who as tenured professors consume considerably more than minimum-wage employees.

Chapter 9

1. This chapter draws heavily from Miranda Perry Fleischer and Daniel Hemel, "The Architecture of a Basic Income," *The University of Chicago Law Review* 87 (2020): 706–8.

2. Felix Salmon, "Universal Basic Income Is Not the Solution to Poverty," *Slate* (July 10, 2018), archived at https://perma.cc/4BT2-7PNL.

Chapter 11

1. This chapter draws heavily from arguments made in Miranda Perry Fleischer and Daniel Hemel, "The Architecture of a Basic Income," *The University of Chicago Law Review* 87 (2020): 669, 696–705.

2. US Census Bureau, *International Database, Population by Age*, archived at https://perma.cc/7QFW-N9RQ.

3. There are 82.6 million who are 19 and under, and 57.8 million people who are 65+. See US Census Bureau, *International Database*.

4. Abby Budiman, Christine Tamir, Lauren Mora, and Luis Noe-Bustamante, *Facts on U.S. Immigrants, 2018,* Pew Research Center (August 20, 2020) (compiling data from chart "Unauthorized Immigrants are almost a quarter of the U.S. foreign-born population"), archived at https://perma.cc/S7BZ-QZZL.

5. For a full list of what Murray proposes to cut, see Charles Murray, *In Our Hands: A Plan to Replace the Welfare State*, 2nd ed. (Washington, DC: AEI Press, 2016), Appendix A.

6. Andy Stern, *Raising the Floor: How a Universal Basic Income Can Renew Our Economy and Rebuild the American Dream* (New York: Public Affairs, 2016), 212.

Chapter 12

1. Tax Foundation estimates are available at Kyle Pomerleau, *Does Andrew Yang's "Freedom Dividend" Proposal Add Up?* (July 24, 2019), archived at https://perma.cc/WDD7-VAQS.
2. Andy Stern, *Raising the Floor: How a Universal Basic Income Can Renew Our Economy and Rebuild the American Dream* (New York: Public Affairs, 2016), 212–3.
3. Miranda Perry Fleischer and Daniel Hemel, "The Architecture of a Basic Income," *The University of Chicago Law Review* 87 (2020): 701.
4. Stern, *Raising the Floor*, 213.
5. A carbon tax would impose a tax on each ton of carbon dioxide released from burning fossil fuels. The suggested size varies by proposal but is typically somewhere between $40 and $100 per ton. Although a carbon tax could be imposed at any point in the production process (for example, either at the oil refinery or at your neighborhood gas pump), producers would pass as much of the additional cost along to consumers as possible. Columbia University SIPA Center on Global Energy Policy, What You Need to Know About a Federal Carbon Tax in the United States, archived at https://perma.cc/7MU9-RLGH.
6. Fleischer and Hemel, "Architecture," 700.
7. For more on data taxes, see Omri Y. Marian, "Taxing Data," *Brigham Young University Law Review* 47 (2021): 511, 560–75; for more on broadband spectrum auctions, see Roslyn Layton, "Spectrum Auctions Have Raised $230 Billion; the FCC's Authority to Conduct Them Will Lapse Soon If Congress Doesn't Act," *Forbes*, April 29, 2022, archived at https://perma.cc/F2MF-XB6P.

Chapter 13

1. This chapter draws heavily from arguments made in Miranda Perry Fleischer and Daniel Hemel, "The Architecture of a Basic Income," *The University of Chicago Law Review* 87 (2020): 679–82.
2. Memorandum from Sasha Gersten-Paal, Dir., Program Dev. Div., Food & Nutrition Serv., U.S. Dept. of Agriculture, to All State Agencies, Supplemental Nutrition Assistance Program, "SNAP—Fiscal Year 2022 Cost-of-Living Adjustments," 2 (August 16, 2021), archived at https://perma.cc/FD4U-DRT7.
3. See *What Are Equivalence Scales?* *2, OECD Project on Income Distribution and Poverty, archived at https://perma.cc/7W3F-GMD4.

Chapter 14

1. This chapter draws heavily from arguments made in Miranda Perry Fleischer and Daniel Hemel, "The Architecture of a Basic Income," *The University of Chicago Law Review* 87 (2020): 675–77.
2. See Fleischer and Hemel, "Architecture," 675.
3. Note that much of this discussion is also applicable to the question of developmentally disabled adults who are dependent upon others for care.
4. Stern, *Raising the Floor: How a Universal Basic Income Can Renew Our Economy and Rebuild the American Dream* (New York: Public Affairs, 2016), 204.

5. See, e.g., Jacob Goldin and Ariel Jurow Kleiman, "Whose Child Is This? Improving Child-Claiming Rules in Safety-Net Programs," *The Yale Law Journal* 131 (2022): 1719.

6. Charles Murray, *In Our Hands: A Plan to Replace the Welfare State*, 2nd ed. (Washington, DC: AEI Press, 2016), 44–47.

7. Compare, for example, Kevin Milligan, "Subsidizing the Stork: New Evidence on Tax Incentives and Fertility," *The Review of Economics and Statistics* 87 (2005): 539, 541–3 (finding a strong fertility effect when Quebec introduced a program that paid up to CAD $8,000 to families for having children), with Jeff Grogger and Stephen G. Bronars, "The Effect of Welfare Payments on the Marriage and Fertility Behavior of Unwed Mothers: Results from a Twins Experiment," *Journal of Political Economy* 109 (2001): 529, 540–2 (finding smaller effects from fertility incentives embedded in various US welfare policies). See also Ioana Marinescu, *No Strings Attached: The Behavioral Effects of U.S. Unconditional Cash Transfer Programs*, NBER Working Paper No. 24337 (2018), 10, available at http://www.nber.org/papers/w24337 (NIT experiments showed either no effect on fertility or a negative one); Janna Bergsvik, Agnes Fauske, and Rannveig K. Hart, "Effects of Policy on Fertility: A Systematic Review of (Quasi)experiments," Statistics Norway Research Department, Discussion Paper No. 922, 25–33 (2020) (temporary but transitory positive effect on fertility rates from universal child transfers; mixed effects from traditional welfare and tax-based cash transfer policies).

Chapter 15

1. A somewhat similar question to the treatment of children and seniors is that of incarcerated individuals. A UBI would likely exclude payments to individuals who are currently incarcerated, on the grounds that their basic needs are already being met. In contrast to many current aid programs, however, a UBI would likely include convicted individuals who have served their time or otherwise paid their debt to society. Excluding such individuals seems contrary to almost all arguments made in favor of a UBI.

2. This chapter draws heavily from arguments made in Miranda Perry Fleischer and Daniel Hemel, "The Architecture of a Basic Income," *The University of Chicago Law Review* 87 (2020): 672–5, 697–8.

3. Social Security Administration, *Annual Statistical Supplement, 2021— Highlights and Trends*, "Old Age, Survivors, and Disability Insurance," archived at https://perma.cc/JNG5-6T4P.

4. Center on Budget and Policy Priorities, *Policy Basics: Top Ten Facts about Social Security* (March 4, 2022), archived at https://perma.cc/5D8M-NSME.

5. See Rick Shenkman, "When Did Social Security Become the Third Rail of American Politics?," *History News Network* (March 6, 2005), https://history newsnetwork.org/article/10522.

6. Fleischer and Hemel, "Architecture," 698.

7. See Social Security Administration, "Retirement Benefits," 12 (2022), archived at https://perma.cc/F7K5-K48Q.

8. In 2020, total SSI payments were roughly $56.3 billion and total SSDI payments were roughly $143.6 billion. SSI Annual Statistical Report, Federal Benefit Rates, Total Annual Payments, and Total Recipients (2020) tbl. 2, archived at https://perma.cc/Q3K9-9XKA; US Social Security Administration, *Annual Statistical Supplement, 2021*.

Chapter 16

1. This discussion draws heavily from arguments made in Miranda Perry Fleischer and Daniel Hemel, "The Architecture of a Basic Income," *The University of Chicago Law Review* 87 (2020): 678–9, 697–8.

2. See Jeremy Ferwerda, Moritz Marbach, and Dominik Hangartner, "Do Immigrants Move to Welfare? Subnational Evidence from Switzerland," *American Journal of Political Science* (2022): 1–17, https://doi.org/10.1111/ajps.12766.

3. See Tanya Broder, Gabrielle Lessard, and Avideh Moussavian, Nat'l Immigration L. Ctr., *Overview of Immigrant Eligibility for Federal Programs* (2021), archived at https://perma.cc/C49R-EDNP. Undocumented immigrant children are eligible for public schooling; undocumented immigrants are entitled to emergency medical assistance; and undocumented immigrants are eligible for a limited set of additional in-kind benefits such as the National School Lunch Program; Special Supplemental Nutrition Program for Women, Infants, and Children (WIC); and Head Start. See Tara Watson, "Do Undocumented Immigrants Overuse Government Benefits?," *EconoFact* (March 28, 2017), archived at https://perma.cc/SFA7-4VBX.

4. In addition, lawful permanent residents who arrived in the United States after August 1996 generally must also work for ten years or serve in the military before becoming eligible for SNAP and SSI (however, children under eighteen years are eligible for SNAP, as are various categories of refugees). See US Department of Agriculture, Food and Nutrition Service, *SNAP Policy on Non-Citizen Eligibility* (September 4, 2013), archived at https://perma.cc/N2K3-DXZW; Social Security Administration, *Spotlight on SSI Benefits for Aliens—2021 Edition*, archived at https://perma.cc/HNU8-WR72.

5. Internal Revenue Service, *Who Qualifies for the Earned Income Tax Credit* (February 2022), archived at https://perma.cc/577H-TRRB; IRS Fact Sheet, "IRS updates the 2021 Child Tax Credit and Advance Child Tax Credit frequently asked questions," Topic M, archived at https://perma.cc/6L9T-DYXX.

6. Philippe Van Parijs and Yannick Vanderborght, *Basic Income: A Radical Proposal for a Free Society and a Sane Economy* (Boston: Harvard University Press, 2017), 222.

7. State of Alaska: Department of Revenue, "Permanent Dividend Fund: Eligibility Requirements," archived at https://perma.cc/SPS8-F5JE. In addition to these residency requirements, Alaska has a few additional rules, such as those relating to criminal sentencing or incarceration during the prior year.

8. Alaska provides some common sense "allowable absences" that do not count as time out of state, such as attending college, serving in the military, receiving medical care, caring for seriously ill family members, and the like.

9. State of Alaska: Department of Revenue, "Permanent Dividend Fund: Absence Guidelines," archived at https://perma.cc/XH5P-HB6D.

Chapter 17

1. This chapter draws heavily from arguments made in Miranda Perry Fleischer and Daniel Hemel, "The Architecture of a Basic Income," *The University of Chicago Law Review* 87 (2020): 685–8.
2. See Amy K. Glasmeier, *Living Wage Calculation for San Francisco County, California* (Living Wage Calculator), archived at https://perma.cc/WZ27-8EHU.
3. See Amy K. Glasmeier, *Living Wage Calculation for Marion County, Indiana* (Living Wage Calculator), archived at https://perma.cc/ARG7-QCWE.
4. See Quoctrung Bui and Claire Cain Miller, "The Typical American Lives Only 18 Miles from Mom," *New York Times* (December 23, 2015), archived at https://perma.cc/A4R7-RRY9.
5. Pawel Krolikowski, Mike Zabek, and Patrick Coate, "Parental Proximity and Earnings After Job Displacements," *Labour Economics* 65 (2020), Article 101877.
6. See Raven Molloy, Christopher L. Smith, and Abigail Wozniak, "Job Changing and the Decline in Long-Distance Migration in the United States," *Demography* 54 (2017): 631, 633 fig 1; United States Census Bureau, *CPS Historical Migration/Geographic Mobility Tables, Table A-1, Annual Geographic Mobility Rates, By Type of Movement, 1948–2021* (November 2021), archived at https://perma.cc/HS3G-XMZG.
7. On the relationship between wages and cost of living across urban areas, see generally Wendell Cox, *The Urban Reform Institute Standard of Living Index, 4th Annual Edition* (December 2020), archived at https://perma.cc/3HFA-PEUZ.
8. See US Department of Labor, Bureau of Labor Statistics, *San Francisco Area Economic Summary* *1 (October 2, 2019), archived at https://perma.cc/U9Q6-PJ9F.
9. The Urban Reform Institute seeks to measure the standard of living across urban areas by adjusting the real average wage for the cost of living. The Washington, DC, area—with high costs but also high wages—comes in first place in this ranking (indicating that workers there can afford more material goods and services than workers elsewhere). See Cox, *Urban Reform Institute Standard of Living Index*, *6 tbl. 1. San Francisco places in the top third. The implication is that larger UBIs for individuals in high-cost-of-living areas might redistribute in the wrong direction (that is, from individuals in places where job prospects are bleak to individuals in places where high-wage employment opportunities are more plentiful).

Chapter 19

1. This chapter draws heavily from arguments made in Miranda Perry Fleischer and Daniel Hemel, "The Architecture of a Basic Income," *The University of Chicago Law Review* 87 (2020): 682–4.
2. See, for example, Matthew Desmond, *Evicted: Poverty and Profit in the American City* (New York: Crown, 2016), 217–8 (one SSI recipient explains her view that using layaway to purchase items like furniture and televisions is a logical alternative to savings since having more than $2,000 in her bank account results in reduced benefits).

3. While higher-net worth individuals would be affected by asset tests in that the test might render them ineligible for benefits, the test would likely not affect their behavior. Once assets exceed the cut-off, the existence of the test no longer matters. There is no disincentive to save more once one is already over the threshold. The incentive effects matter near the threshold, and it is far more likely low-income households will be the ones near the threshold.

Chapter 20

1. This chapter draws on arguments made in Miranda Perry Fleischer and Daniel Hemel, "The Architecture of a Basic Income," *The University of Chicago Law Review* 87 (2020): 688–90.
2. Bruce Ackerman and Anne Alstott, *The Stakeholder Society* (New Haven, CT: Yale University Press, 2000).
3. Juliana Uhurua Bidadanure, "The Political Theory of Universal Basic Income," *Annual Review of Political Science* 22 (2019): 481–501; *Yang 2020: The Freedom Dividend*, archived at https://perma.cc/6GFD-NSSE.
4. Imagine a $500-per-month UBI. Borrowing $5,800 today and assigning one's next twelve UBI payments to the lender is roughly the equivalent of borrowing at a 6.3% interest rate. Presumably, lenders would offer an amount less than the nominal sum of future payments to reflect (a) the time value of money and (b) the risk that the borrower will die before the loan is repaid. These calculations are from Fleischer and Hemel, "Architecture," 688.
5. This raises the further question of whether individuals like *Bonnie* should be bailed out later if they find themselves in dire circumstances. We address this more in chapter 56.
6. Philippe Van Parijs and Yannick Vanderborght, *Basic Income: A Radical Proposal for a Free Society and a Sane Economy* (Boston: Harvard University Press, 2017), 10.
7. See Fleischer and Hemel, "Architecture," 688–90.
8. Existing welfare programs have contradictory rules on this point. For example, some Social Security benefits are garnishable for child support, while some are not. The IRS generally cannot seize Social Security or welfare benefits for back taxes, but the EITC can be seized if a borrower defaults on a student loan.
9. For more on the issue of garnishment, see Matthew Adam Bruckner, "Debtor/Creditor Issues with Basic Income Guarantees," *American Bankruptcy Institute Law Review* 29 (2021): 171.

Chapter 21

1. This chapter draws heavily from arguments made in Miranda Perry Fleischer and Daniel Hemel, "The Architecture of a Basic Income," *The University of Chicago Law Review* 87 (2020): 692–5.
2. Jesse M. Shapiro, "Is There a Daily Discount Rate? Evidence from the Food Stamp Nutrition Cycle," *Journal of Public Economics* 89 (2005): 303, 307–8; Karen S. Hamrick and Margaret Andrews, "SNAP Participants' Eating Patterns over the Benefit Month: A Time Use Perspective," *PLOS ONE* 11 (2016): 1, 14 fig 2. Some evidence also suggests that stores respond to this cycle by raising prices on the day that SNAP benefits are paid. See Justine

Hastings and Ebonya Washington, "The First of the Month Effect: Consumer Behavior and Store Responses," *American Economic Journal: Economic Policy* 2 (2010): 142, 156–9.

3. See, for example, United States Department of Agriculture, Economic Research Service, *Informing Food and Nutrition Assistance Policy: 10 Years of Research at ERS* 30 (December 2007); Tommy Tobin, "Semi-Monthly Benefit Transfers Are a Simple Way to Improve Food Stamps," *Forbes* (April 23, 2018), archived at https://perma.cc/4WEN-6PVJ.

4. Michelle Lyon Drumbl, *Tax Credits for the Working Poor: A Call for Reform* (New York: Cambridge University Press, 2019), 31.

5. Steve Holt, *Periodic Payment of the Earned Income Tax Credit Revisited* (Brookings Metropolitan Policy Program, December 2015), 4–5, archived at https://perma.cc/CHN4-5C3H.

6. Drumbl, *Tax Credits*.

Chapter 22

1. This chapter draws heavily from arguments made in Miranda Perry Fleischer and Daniel Hemel, "The Architecture of a Basic Income," *The University of Chicago Law Review* 87 (2020): 695–6.

2. See Social Security Administration, *Annual Statistical Supplement to the Social Security Bulletin, 2021* *2–3 (December 2021), archived at https://perma.cc/AAC6-4KXZ.

3. See Social Security Administration, Office of the Inspector General, *Unauthorized My Social Security Direct Deposit Changes Through May 2018* (September 2019), archived at https://perma.cc/KRY7-6X86.

4. Erica York, *Census Data Shows Households Saved Economic Impact Payments* (July 13, 2021), archived at https://perma.cc/7ZL4-VNB3.

5. Internal Revenue Service, "Returns Filed, Taxes Collected & Refunds Issued" (visited March 3, 2022), archived at https://perma.cc/RL3X-V9CR.

6. See, for example, Michael Munger, "One and One-Half Cheers for a Basic Income Guarantee: We Could Do Worse, and Already Have," *Independent Review* 19 (2015): 503, 506.

7. See Social Security Administration, *Monthly Statistical Snapshot, July 2018* *1 tbl. 1, archived at https://perma.cc/BJG5-7MLZ.

8. See "Public Expresses Favorable Views of a Number of Federal Agencies," Pew Research Center (October 1, 2019), archived at https://perma.cc/74RT-DYL7; *Beyond Distrust: How Americans View Their Government* *58–59, *Pew Research Center* (November 23, 2015), archived at https://perma.cc/J3FV-NTHX.

9. See Leandra Lederman, "IRS Reform: Politics as Usual?," *Columbia Journal of Tax Law* 7 (2016): 36, 48–55.

Chapter 23

1. This chapter draws heavily from arguments made in Miranda Perry Fleischer and Daniel Hemel, "The Architecture of a Basic Income," *The University of Chicago Law Review* 87 (2020): 691–2.

2. See Social Security Administration, *Social Security Administration Beneficiaries: Social Security Direct Deposit and Check Statistics* (August 2019), archived at https://perma.cc/65CM-3MR6.

3. Internal Revenue Service, "Get Your Refund Faster: Tell IRS to Direct Deposit your Refund to One, Two, or Three Accounts" (January 6, 2022), archived at https://perma.cc/4RVC-DAN9.

4. Kavitha George, "Here's when Alaskans can expect to get this year's PFD," Alaska Public Media (September 22, 2021), archived at https://perma.cc/7CQN-ADLQ.

5. See Leora Klapper, *Can Universal Basic Income Boost Financial Inclusion and Transparency?* (Brookings Institute: Future Development, June 15, 2017), archived at https://perma.cc/68YZ-WA2W.

6. Klapper, *Can Universal Basic Income.*

7. See, for example, Alicia Naumoff, *Why Universal Basic Income Should Be Paid in Bitcoin* (Cointelegraph, Jan 19, 2017), archived at https://perma.cc/3KBD-88M7.

8. https://www.hedgeforhumanity.org/.

9. https://democracy.earth/.

Chapter 25

1. See California Women Infants and Children Program, "California WIC Authorized Food List Shopping Guide" (April 2, 2019), archived at https://perma.cc/E87P-UCN6.

2. See 42 USC § 608(a)(12)(A)(i)–(iii). The law does not use the term "strip club" but instead refers to "any retail establishment which provides adult-oriented entertainment in which performers disrobe or perform in an unclothed state for entertainment." 42 USC § 608(a)(12)(A)(iii).

3. See Kan. Stat. Ann. § 39-709(b)(14).

4. The following discussion draws from Miranda Perry Fleischer and Daniel Hemel, "Atlas Nods: The Libertarian Case for a Basic Income," *Wisconsin Law Review* (2017): 1234–7.

Chapter 26

1. This discussion draws on Miranda Perry Fleischer and Daniel Hemel, "The Architecture of a Basic Income," *The University of Chicago Law Review* 87 (2020): 656–8.

2. See Jennifer L. Erkulwater, *Disability Rights and the American Social Safety Net* (Ithaca, NY: Cornell University Press, 2006), 129–31; Social Security Administration, *Annual Statistics Report on the Social Security Disability Insurance Program, 2016*, at 25 tbl.6 (Oct. 2017), https://www.ssa.gov/policy/docs/statcomps/di_asr/2016/di_asr16.pdf; Social Security Administration, *SSI Annual Statistical Report, 2016*, at 76 tbl. 38 (November 2017), https://www.ssa.gov/policy/docs/statcomps/ssi_asr/2016/ssi_as r16.pdf; Social Security Administration, *SSI Annual Statistical Report, 2017*, at 76 tbl. 38 (September 2018), archived at http://perma.cc/SPN9-883L.

3. On the disagreement among the Social Security Administration, the IRS, and the courts, see American Bar Association Section of Taxation, "Comments on Information Collection Under Revenue Procedure 99-21," at 13–17 (February 1, 2018), archived at https://perma.cc/9WCM-SMZ2.

4. See Hugo Benitez-Silva, Moshe Buchinsky, and John Rust, *How Large Are the Classification Errors in the Social Security Disability Award Process?*, NBER Working Paper No. 10219 (Jan. 2004), 5–6, 48 (summarizing past research and re-estimating false negative rate based on new methodology), archived at https://perma.cc/S55Z-LYRP.
5. See Social Security Administration, *What's New in 2022?*, archived at https://perma.cc/S9RY-L28Y. For more on the various disability programs in the United States and their eligibility requirements and rules, see Social Security Administration, *Red Book: A Summary Guide to Employment Supports for People with Disabilities under the Social Security Disability Insurance (SSDI) and Supplemental Security Income (SSI) Programs*, archived at https://perma.cc/3L3P-H4D8.

Chapter 27

1. H. Immervoll and M. Pearson, "A Good Time for Making Work Pay? Taking Stock of In-Work Benefits and Related Measures across the OECD," *OECD Social, Employment and Migration Working Papers* (2009), No. 81, OECD Publishing, Paris, https://doi.org/10.1787/225442803245.
2. Immervoll and Pearson, "A Good Time."
3. See Kerry Ryan, "EITC as Income (In)Stability," *Florida Tax Review* 15 (2014): 583.
4. Immervoll and Pearson, "A Good Time."
5. Internal Revenue Service, Revenue Procedure 2019-44 (2019).
6. Philippe Van Parijs and Yannick Vanderborght, *Basic Income: A Radical Proposal for a Free Society and a Sane Economy* (Cambridge, MA: Harvard University Press, 2017), 40–43; Immervoll and Pearson, "A Good Time."
7. Internal Revenue Service Publication 596, *Earned Income Credit (EIC)*, archived at https://perma.cc/RC3P-AHTN.
8. Estimates of the number of returns claiming overpayments range from 20% to 30%, with estimates of the annual dollar amount of overpayments ranging from $8.6 billion to $18.4 billion. See Michelle Lyon Drumbl, *Tax Credits for the Working Poor: A Call for Reform* (New York: Cambridge University Press, 2019), 29, 46.
9. Drumbl, *Tax Credits*, 29.

Chapter 28

1. See Sweden—Employment, Social Affairs & Inclusion—European Commission, archived at https://perma.cc/GYX6-4MBN; Applying for family allowance—Citizens—Guichet.lu—Administrative Guide—Luxembourg, archived at https://perma.cc/66AZ-QLV6; Financial Support Bundesagentur für Arbeit., archived at https://perma.cc/6LQ4-GQBQ; Service-public.fr, 2022, Family allowances, archived at https://perma.cc/G3Q3-D8PJ; Citizens Information, Child Benefit, archived at https://perma.cc/LZ7S-Q2Y7.
2. Lauren E. Jones, Kevin Milligan, and Mark Stabile, "Child Cash Benefits and Family Expenditures: Evidence from the National Child Benefit," *Canadian Journal of Economics* 52, no. 4 (November 2019): 1433–63.
3. G. B. Dahl and L. Lochner, "The impact of family income on child achievement: Evidence from the Earned Income Tax Credit," *The American Economic Review* 102, no. 5 (2012): 1927–56; Kevin Milligan and Mark Stabile, "Do Child Tax Benefits Affect the Well-being of Children? Evidence from

Canadian Child Benefit Expansions," *American Economic Journal: Economic Policy* 3, no. 3 (August 2011): 175–205; Raj Chetty, John N. Friedman, and Jonah Rockoff, "New Evidence on the Long-Term Impacts of Tax Credits," *Proceedings, Annual Conference on Taxation and Minutes of the Annual Meeting of the National Tax Association* 104 (2011): 116–24.

4. Jacob Bastian and Katherine Michelmore, "The Long-Term Impact of the Earned Income Tax Credit on Children's Education and Employment Outcomes," *Journal of Labor Economics* 36 (2018): 1127–63.

5. See Irwin Garfinkel, Laurel Sariscsany, Elizabeth Ananat, Sophie M. Collyer, Robert Paul Hartley, Buyi Wang, and Christopher Wimer, *The Benefits and Costs of a US Child Allowance*, NBER Working Paper No. 29854 (March 2022), 8–23 (collecting studies); Bastian and Michelmore, "Long-Term Impact," 1127–63.

6. Hilary Hoynes, Martha Bailey, Maya Rossin-Slater, and Reed Walker, *Is the Social Safety Net a Long-Term Investment? Large-Scale Evidence from the Food Stamps Program*, NBER Working Paper No. 26942 (2020), 3–4.

7. Hilary W. Hoynes, Douglas L. Miller, and David Simon, *Linking EITC Outcomes to Real Health Outcomes*, Policy Brief, Center for Poverty Research V. 1 No. 2.

8. See Randall K. Q. Akee, William E. Copeland, Gordon Keeler, Adrian Angold, and E. Jane Costello, "Parents' Incomes and Children's Outcomes: A Quasi-Experiment Using Transfer Payments from Casino Profits," *American Economic Journal: Applied Economics* 2 (2010): 86.

9. For a summary of studies of cash and near cash transfer programs, see Irwin Garfinkel, Laurel Sariscsany, Elizabeth Ananat, Sophie Collyer, Buyi Wang, Robert Harley, and Christopher Wimer, *The Benefits and Costs of a Child Allowance*, Poverty and Social Policy Brief, V. 5. No. 1 (2021).

10. See, e.g., Jason DeParle, "Monthly Payments to Families with Children to Begin," *New York Times* (July 12, 2021), archived at https://perma.cc/CN7A-VRZX. ("When Fresh EBT asked users about their spending plans, the answers differed from those about the stimulus checks. 'We saw more responses specifically related to kids—school clothes, school supplies, a toddler bed . . . the framing of the benefit matters.'")

11. Shelly J. Lundberg, Robert A. Pollak, and Terence J. Wales, "Do Husbands and Wives Pool Their Resources? Evidence from the United Kingdom Child Benefit," *The Journal of Human Resources* 32, no. 3 (Summer 1997): 463–80; Jennifer Ward-Batts, "Out of the Wallet and into the Purse: Using Micro Data to Test Income Pooling," *The Journal of Human Resources* 43, no. 2 (2008): 325–51.

Chapter 29

1. See Milton Friedman, *Capitalism and Freedom* (Chicago: University of Chicago Press, 1962).

2. Milton Friedman and Rose Friedman, *Free To Choose: A Personal Statement* (New York: Harcourt, Inc., 1980), 120–1.

3. Much of this chapter, including these examples, is drawn from Miranda Perry Fleischer and Daniel Hemel, "Atlas Nods: The Libertarian Case for a Basic Income," *Wisconsin Law Review* (2017): 1189, and Miranda Perry Fleischer and Daniel Hemel, "The Architecture of a Basic Income," *The University of Chicago Law Review* 87 (2020): 637–8.

4. There may also be administrative differences, as addressed elsewhere in this book, such as payment frequency (see chapter 21) and which agencies would be tapped to administer each program (see chapter 22).

Chapter 30

1. Thomas Paine, "Agrarian Justice (1797)," in *The Origins of Universal Grants* (Basingstoke and New York: Springer, 2004) 15–16 (Paine wrote "Agrarian Justice" in 1795–1796, but it was not published in English until 1797).
2. Other recent advocates of similar proposals include James Tobin (1968), William Klein (1977), and Robert Haveman (1988).
3. Adjusted for inflation, $80,000 is just over $132,000 in 2021 dollars. Author's calculation using https://www.bls.gov/data/inflation_calculator.htm.
4. Philippe Van Parijs and Yannick Vanderborght, *Basic Income: A Radical Proposal for a Free Society and a Sane Economy* (Boston: Harvard University Press, 2017), 258.
5. European Commission, Employment, Social Affairs & Inclusion, *Belgium—Family Benefits*, archived at https://perma.cc/84A9-TQ5G.
6. American Opportunity Accounts Act, S. 222, 117th Congress (2021–2022); Cory Booker, *Booker Announces New Bill Aimed at Combating Wealth Inequality*, archived at https://perma.cc/YT9C-8X86.
7. See Miranda Perry Fleischer and Daniel Hemel, "Atlas Nods: The Libertarian Case for a Basic Income," *Wisconsin Law Review* (2017): 1241–4 and Miranda Perry Fleischer and Daniel Hemel, "The Architecture of a Basic Income," *The University of Chicago Law Review* 87 (2020): 688–90.
8. Bruce Ackerman and Anne Alstott, *The Stakeholder Society* (New Haven, CT: Yale University Press, 2000), 24.
9. Ackerman and Allstot, *The Stakeholder Society*, 191.
10. Van Parijs and Vanderborght, *Basic Income*, 31.
11. Van Parijs and Vanderborght, *Basic Income*, 31.
12. Van Parijs and Vanderborght, *Basic Income*, 31; Bruce Ackerman, Anne Alstott, and Philippe Van Parijs, *Redesigning Redistribution: Basic Income and Stakeholder Grants as Cornerstones for an Egalitarian Capitalism* (New York: Verso, 2006), 159.
13. See Fleischer and Hemel, "Atlas Nods," 1242; Fleischer and Hemel, "Architecture," 689.

Chapter 31

1. For one such proposal, see Mark Paul, William Darity, and Darrick Hamilton, "The Federal Job Guarantee—A Policy to Achieve Permanent Full Employment," *Policy Futures* (Washington, DC: Center on Budget and Policy Priorities, March 9, 2018).
2. A helpful overview of some of the non-monetary benefits of work can be found in Anna Gheaus and Lisa Herog, "The Goods of Work (Other Than Money!)," *Journal of Social Philosophy* 47, no. 1 (Spring 2016): 70–89. See also Cholbi, Michael, "Philosophical Approaches to Work and Labor," *The Stanford Encyclopedia of Philosophy* (Fall 2022 Edition), Edward N. Zalta and Uri Nodelman (eds.), https://plato.stanford.edu/archives/fall2022/entries/work-labor/, especially section 2.1.
3. Andy Stern, *Raising the Floor: How a Universal Basic Income Can Renew Our Economy and Rebuild the American Dream* (PublicAffairs, 2016), 165.
4. See Jon Elster, "Is There (or Should There Be) a Right to Work?," in *Democracy and the Welfare State*, ed. Amy Gutmann (Princeton University Press, 2021), 53–78.

Chapter 32

1. Matthew Berman and Random Reamey, *Permanent Fund Dividends and Poverty in Alaska* (Anchorage, AK: Institute of Social and Economic Research, University of Alaska Anchorage, November 2016), https://iseralaska.org/static/legacy_publication_links/2016_12-PFDandPoverty.pdf.

2. Wankyo Chung, Hyungserk Ha, and Beomsoo Kim, "Money Transfer and Birth Weight: Evidence from the Alaska Permanent Fund Dividend," *Economic Inquiry* 54, no. 1 (2016): 576–90 .

3. Paul Harstad, *Executive Summary of Findings from a Survey of Alaska Voters on the PFD* (Harstad Strategic Research, June 22, 2017) .

4. Jay Hammond, *Tales of Alaska's Bush Rat Governor* (Kenmore, WA: Epicenter Press, 1996), 254.

Chapter 33

1. Milton Friedman, *Capitalism and Freedom*, 40th Anniversary (Chicago: University of Chicago, 2002).

2. Jyotsna Sreenivasan, ed., "A Statement by Economists on Income Guarantees and Supplements," in *Poverty and the Government in America* (Santa Barbara, CA: ABC-CLIO, 2009), 269.

3. Gilbert Yale Steiner, *The State of Welfare* (Brookings Institution, 1971), 96.

4. Robert Spiegelman and K. E. Yaeger, "Overview (of the Special Issue, The Seattle and Denver Income Maintenance Experiments)," *The Journal of Human Resources* 15, no. 4 (Fall 1980): 463–79.

5. Gary Burtless, "The Work Response to a Guaranteed Income: A Survey of Experimental Evidence," in *Conference Series [Proceedings]*, vol. 30 (Federal Reserve Bank of Boston, 1986), 22–59. For a more recent helpful critical overview of the experiments, see Karl Widerquist, "A Failure to Communicate: What (If Anything) Can We Learn from the Negative Income Tax Experiments?," *The Journal of Socio-Economics* 34, no. 1 (2005): 49–81, https://doi.org/10.1016/j.socec.2004.09.050.

6. R. A. Levine, H. Watts, R. Hollister, W. Williams, A. O'Connor, and K. Widerquist, "A Retrospective on the Negative Income Tax Experiments," in ed. Karl Widerquist, Michael Anthony Lewis, and Steven Pressman, *The Ethics and Economics of the Basic Income Guarantee* (Abingdon and New York: Routledge, 2005), 99.

7. Spiegelman and Yaeger, "Overview (of the Special Issue: The Seattle and Denver Income Maintenance Experiments)."

Chapter 34

1. See, for an overview, Evelyn L. Forget, "The Town with No Poverty: The Health Effects of a Canadian Guaranteed Annual Income Field Experiment," *Canadian Public Policy* 37, no. 3 (2011): 283–305; Evelyn L. Forget, *Basic Income for Canadians: From the COVID-19 Emergency to Financial Security for All* (Toronto: James Lorimer & Company, 2020), chapter 2.

2. See Mohammad Ferdosi, Tom McDowell, Wayne Lewchuk, and Stephanie Ross, *Southern Ontario's Basic Income Experience* (Hamilton: Hamilton Community Foundation, Hamilton Roundtable for Poverty Reduction and Labour Studies at McMaster University, March 2020), https://labourstudies.mcmaster.ca/documents/southern-ontarios-basic-income-experience.pdf. Accessed July 3, 2022.

Chapter 35

1. Myron J. Frankman, "Making the Difference! The BIG in Namibia: Basic Income Grant Pilot Project Assessment Report, April 2009," *Canadian Journal of Development Studies/Revue Canadienne d'études Du Développement* 29, no. 3–4 (2010): 526–9.
2. Guy Standing, "Unconditional Basic Income: Two Pilots in Madhya Pradesh," in *A Background Note Prepared for the Delhi Conference* (Delhi, 2013).
3. Abhijit Banerjee, Michael Faye, Alan Krueger, Paul Niehaus, and Tavneet Suri, "Effects of a Universal Basic Income during the Pandemic" (2022), 55, https://econweb.ucsd.edu/~pniehaus/papers/ubi_covid.pdf.
4. See https://www.givedirectly.org/ubi-study/.

Chapter 36

1. Dylan Matthews, "Finland's Hugely Exciting Experiment in Basic Income, Explained," *Vox* (December 8, 2015), https://www.vox.com/2015/12/8/9872554/finland-basic-income-experiment.
2. Jimmy O'Donnell, "Why Basic Income Failed in Finland," *Jacobin* (December 1, 2019), https://jacobin.com/2019/12/basic-income-finland-experiment-kela.
3. Kela, "Preliminary Results of the Basic Income Experiment" (August 2, 2019), https://www.epressi.com/tiedotteet/hallitus-ja-valtio/prelimin ary-results-of-the-basic-income-experiment-les-resultats-preliminaires-de-lexperience-du-revenu-de-basepredvariteljnye-rezuljtaty-eksperimentalj noj-koncepcii-bezuslovnogovorlaufige-ergebnisse-des-experiments-zum-gru ndeinkommen.html.
4. "Employment," SEED, accessed June 6, 2022, https://www.stocktondemons tration.org/employment.
5. http://mayorsforagi.org.

Chapter 37

1. A more in-depth discussion of what can and cannot be learned from UBI experiments can be found in Karl Widerquist, *A Critical Analysis of Basic Income Experiments for Researchers, Policymakers, and Citizens* (Cham: Palgrave, 2018).

Chapter 38

1. Andrew Yang, *Yang 2020: The Freedom Dividend*, archived at https://perma. cc/6GFD-NSSE.
2. Wil Hunt, Sudipa Sarkar, and Chris Warhurst, "Measuring the Impact of AI on Jobs at the Organization Level: Lessons from a Survey of UK Business Leaders," *Research Policy* 51, no. 2 (March 1, 2022): 104425, https://doi.org/10.1016/j.respol.2021.104425.
3. Max Roser, "Employment in Agriculture," *Our World In Data* (2013). Retrieved from: https://ourworldindata.org/employment-in-agriculture.

Chapter 39

1. Emily A. Shrider, Melissa Kollar, Frances Chen, and Jessica Semega, *Income and Poverty in the United States: 2020* (U.S. Census Bureau Report P60-273, 2021), archived at https://perma.cc/M58S-V79H.
2. See World Bank Blogs, *April 2022 Global Poverty Update from the World Bank* (World Bank), 13, archived at https://perma.cc/P6UG-TN4F.

3. Andy Stern, *Raising the Floor: How a Universal Basic Income Can Renew Our Economy and Rebuild the American Dream* (New York: Public Affairs, 2016), 170.

4. Andrew Yang, *Yang 2020: The Freedom Dividend*, archived at https://perma.cc/6GFD-NSSE.

5. Chris Hughes, *Fair Shot: Rethinking Inequality and How We Earn* (New York: St. Martin's Press, 2018), 5. Technically, Hughes's plan is not a true UBI, since it contains a work requirement, but it is often discussed alongside other prominent UBI proposals.

6. US Department of Health and Human Services, Office of the Assistant Secretary for Planning and Evaluation, "HHS Poverty Guidelines for 2022" (January 12, 2022), archived at https://perma.cc/6LXZ-K8LU.

7. The following discussion draws from Miranda Perry Fleischer and Daniel Hemel, "The Architecture of a Basic Income," *The University of Chicago Law Review* 87 (2020): 666–8. See also Daniel Hemel, "Bringing the Basic Income Back to Earth," *The New Rambler* (September 19, 2016), archived at https://perma.cc/H7MS-FLXW.

Chapter 40

1. See Juliana Menasce Horowitz, Ruth Igielink, and Rakesh Kochhar, *Trends in Income and Wealth Inequality*, Pew Research Center (2020), archived at https://perma.cc/4MMV-X6KF.

2. See Raj Chetty, Nathaniel Hendren, David Grusky, Maximilian Hell, Robert Manduca, and Jimmy Narang, "The Fading American Dream: Trends in Absolute Income Mobility Since 1940," *Science* 356, no. 6336 (2017): 398–406.

3. Tax Policy Center, "Household Income Quintiles" (January 25, 2022), archived at https://perma.cc/M75A-2GZN.

4. See Kristin F. Butcher, *Assessing the Long-Run Benefits of Transfers to Low-Income Families*, Hutchins Center on Fiscal & Monetary Policy at Brookings Working Paper (2017), archived at https://perma.cc/V9XD-V3JV.

Chapter 41

1. This discussion draws from Miranda Perry Fleischer and Daniel Hemel, "Atlas Nods: The Libertarian Case for a Basic Income," *Wisconsin Law Review* (2017): 1234–7.

2. These statistics are from Michael Tanner, "The Pros and Cons of a Guaranteed National Income," *Cato Institute* (May 12, 2015), 1, 7, archived at https://perma.cc/3GN4-2L6B.

3. Kevin D. Williamson, "The White Ghetto," *National Review* (January 9, 2014), archived at https://perma.cc/BN3D-2Y5J.

4. See Teresa A. Coughlin, Sharon K. Long, Lisa Clemens-Cope, and Dean Resnick, *What Difference Does Medicaid Make? Assessing Cost Effectiveness, Access, and Financial Protection under Medicaid for Low-Income Adults*, KFF.org (May 2013), archived at https://perma.cc/697L-8BJN.

Chapter 42

1. See D. James Greiner and Cassandra Wolos Pattanayak, "Randomized Evaluation in Legal Assistance: What Difference Does Representation (Offer and Actual Use) Make?," *Yale Law Journal* 121 (2012): 2118, 2192.

Chapter 43

1. Aditya Aladangady and Akila Forde, "Wealth Inequality and the Racial Wealth Gap," *FEDS Notes* (October 22, 2021), https://www.federalreserve.gov/econres/notes/feds-notes/wealth-inequality-and-the-racial-wealth-gap-20211022.htm.

2. Moritz Kuhn, Moritz Schularick, and Ulrike Steins, *Income and Wealth Inequality in America, 1949–2016* (Institute Working Papers, June 14, 2018), https://www.minneapolisfed.org:443/research/institute-working-papers/income-and-wealth-inequality-in-america-1949-2016.

3. Liz Mineo, "Racial Wealth Gap May Be a Key to Other Inequities," *Harvard Gazette* (blog) (June 3, 2021), https://news.harvard.edu/gazette/story/2021/06/racial-wealth-gap-may-be-a-key-to-other-inequities/.

4. Alex Kasprak, "Is Oakland Offering 'Guaranteed Income' Only to People of Color?," *Snopes.com* (April 5, 2021), https://www.snopes.com/fact-check/oakland-guaranteed-income-bipoc/.

5. For discussion, see Jhumpa Bhattacharya, *Exploring Guaranteed Income through a Racial and Gender Justice Lens* (Roosevelt Institute Issue Brief, June 2019).

6. See Joe Soss, Stanford F. Schram, Thomas V. Vartanian, and Erin O'Brien, "Setting the Terms of Relief: Explaining State Policy Choices in the Devolution Revolution," *American Journal of Political Science* 45, no. 2 (2001): 378–95.

Chapter 44

1. See Charles Murray, *In Our Hands: A Plan to Replace the Welfare State*, 2nd ed. (Washington, DC: AEI Press, 2016), 44, 47.

2. See chapter 14 n. 7.

3. Robert A. Levine, Harold Watts, Robinson Hollister, Walter Williams, Alice O'Connor, and Karl Widerquist, "A Retrospective on the Negative Income Tax Experiments," in *The Ethics and Economics of the Basic Income Guarantee* (Ashgate: 2005), 99.

Chapter 45

1. Charles A. Murray, *In Our Hands: A Plan to Replace the Welfare State* (Washington, DC: AEI Press, 2006), 81.

2. Alexis de Tocqueville, *Democracy in America* (1835; repr., Indianapolis, IN: Liberty Fund, 1969).

3. For an overview, see David Beito, *From Mutual Aid to the Welfare State: Fraternal Societies and Social Services, 1890–1967* (Chapel Hill: University of North Carolina Press, 1999).

4. Murray, *In Our Hands*, 85–86.

5. Robert D. Putnam, *Bowling Alone: The Collapse and Revival of American Community* (New York: Simon & Schuster, 2000).

Chapter 46

1. David Graeber, *Bullshit Jobs: A Theory* (New York: Simon and Schuster, 2019).

2. Andy Stern, *Raising the Floor: How a Universal Basic Income Can Renew Our Economy and Rebuild the American Dream* (PublicAffairs, 2016), 188.

3. Jason Furman, "Occupational Licensing and Economic Rents," *The Brookings Institution* (2015, November 2), https://www.brookings.edu/wp-content/uploads/2015/10/20151102_furman_licensing_presentation.pdf.

Chapter 47

1. Green Party Platform, July 2020, https://www.gp.org/economic_justice_and_sustainability/#ejLivableIncome. Accessed June 20, 2022.

Chapter 48

1. Miranda Perry Fleischer and Daniel Hemel, "The Architecture of a Basic Income," *The University of Chicago Law Review* 87 (2020): 669.

Chapter 49

1. We have chosen $35 as an easy illustration; a recent report estimates that for most households, an additional $100 in income would result in reduced benefits of $24 to $36. See Elizabeth Wolkimir and Lexin Cai, *The Supplemental Nutrition Assistance Program Includes Earnings Incentives* (June 5, 2019), archived at https://perma.cc/4AHC-FCZQ.
2. See Congressional Budget Office, *Effective Marginal Tax Rates for Low- and Moderate-Income Workers in 2016* (November 2015), archived at https://perma.cc/S3X3-9YMH.
3. See chapter 26.
4. See Damon Jones and Ioana Marinescu, "The Labor Market Impacts of Universal and Permanent Cash Transfers: Evidence from the Alaska Permanent Fund," *American Economic Journal: Economic Policy* 14, no. 2 (2022): 329 (finding no effect on employment levels and an increase in part-time employment that could be due either to workers working fewer hours or new entrants into the part-time labor force).
5. See Jones and Marinescu, "Labor Market Impacts."

Chapter 50

1. John Rawls, *A Theory of Justice*, 1st ed. (Cambridge: Belknap Press, 1971).
2. See, for an overview, Karl Widerquist, "Reciprocity and the Guaranteed Income," *Politics and Society* 27, no. 3 (1999): 386–401.
3. John Kenneth Galbraith, "The Speculative Bubble Always Comes to an End—and Never in a Pleasant or Peaceful Way. Interview with Elizabeth Mehren," *Los Angeles Times* (December 12, 1999), https://latimesblogs.latimes.com/thedailymirror/2008/10/voices——john.html.

Chapter 51

1. Myron J. Frankman, "Making the Difference! The BIG in Namibia; Basic Income Grant Pilot Project Assessment Report, April 2009," *Canadian Journal of Development Studies/Revue Canadienne d'études Du Développement* 29, no. 3–4 (2010): 526–9.
2. See, e.g., Johannes Haushofer and Jeremy Shapiro, *Policy Brief: Impacts of Unconditional Cash Transfers* (2013): 2; Esther Schuering, *Social Cash Transfers in Zambia: A Work in Progress*, in Degol Hailu and Fabio Veras Soeres, eds., *Cash Transfers: Lessons from Africa and Latin America* (2008).
3. David K. Evans and Anna Popova, *Cash Transfers and Temptation Goods: A Review of Global Evidence*, World Bank Policy Research Working Paper No. 6886 (2014), 3.

4. Abhijit Banerjee, Michael Faye, Alan Krueger, Paul Niehaus, and Tavneet Suri, "Effects of a Universal Basic Income during the Pandemic" (2022), 16, https://econweb.ucsd.edu/~pniehaus/papers/ubi_covid.pdf.

5. See chapter 35.

6. Hilary W. Hoynes, Douglas L. Miller, and David Simon, *Linking EITC Outcomes to Real Health Outcomes*, Policy Brief, Center for Poverty Research V. 1 No. 2.

7. See Randall K. Q. Akee, William E. Copeland, Gordon Keeler, Adrian Angold, and E. Jane Costello, "Parents' Incomes and Children's Outcomes: A Quasi-Experiment Using Transfer Payments from Casino Profits," *American Economic Journal: Applied Economics* 2 (2010): 86.

8. See Irwin Garfinkel, Laurel Sariscsany, Elizabeth Ananat, Sophie Collyer, Robert Hartley, Buyi Wang, and Christopher Wimer, *The Costs and Benefits of a Child Allowance*, Poverty and Social Policy Brief, V. 5. No. 1 (2021).

Chapter 52

1. Much of this discussion is drawn from Miranda Perry Fleischer and Daniel Hemel, "Atlas Nods: The Libertarian Case for a Basic Income," *Wisconsin Law Review* (2017): 1247–48.

2. See, e.g., Chesterfield Polkey, *Most States Have Ended SNAP Ban for Convicted Drug Felons*, National Conference of State Legislatures (July 30, 2019), archived at https://perma.cc/5L53-EC6Z (discussing limits on SNAP participation imposed on those convicted of drug felonies).

Chapter 53

1. San Diego County Housing and Community Development Services, *Rental Assistance*, archived at https://perma.cc/3YUD-WNLE.

2. For more on this point, see Daniel Hemel, "Bringing the Basic Income Back to Earth," *The New Rambler* (September 19, 2016), archived at https://perma.cc/H7MS-FLXW.

3. US Department of Agriculture, "SNAP–Fiscal Year 2022 Cost-of-Living Adjustments" (August 16, 2021), archived at https://perma.cc/7JYM-4EX4; Internal Revenue Service, "Earned Income and Earned Income Tax Credit (EITC) Tables," archived at https://perma.cc/PN9W-7ACX; Internal Revenue Service, "Tax Year 2021/Filing Season 2022 Child Tax Credit Frequently Asked Questions," archived at https://perma.cc/4AE9-A8D9; Special Supplemental Nutrition Program for Women, Infants and Children (WIC) Program Data Table (March 2022), archived at https://perma.cc/B3BL-FBHG.

4. Center on Budget and Policy Priorities, *Policy Basics: Top Ten Facts about Social Security* (March 4, 2022), archived at https://perma.cc/5D8M-NSME.

Chapter 55

1. Damon Jones and Ioana Marinescu, "Universal Cash Transfers and Inflation," *National Tax Journal* 75, no. 2 (September 2022): 628–30.

2. Jones and Marinescu, "Universal Cash Transfers."

3. Ugo Gentilini, Margaret Grosh, and Ruslan Yemtsov, "The Idea of a Universal Basic Income," in *Exploring Universal Basic Income: A Guide to Navigating Concepts, Evidence, and Practices*, eds. Ugo Gentilini et al., (Washington, D.C.: World Bank Publications, 2019).

4. Jones and Marinescu, "Universal Cash Transfers," 651.

5. See Francois de Soyres, Ana Maria Santacreu, and Henry Young, "Demand-Supply Imbalance during the Covid-19 Pandemic: The Role of Fiscal Policy," *Federal Reserve Bank of St. Louis Review* 105, no. 1 (Q1 2023).

6. A minority view, held by those who subscribe to modern monetary theory (MMT), is that increasing the amount of money in circulation is not inflationary as long as the overall amount of money in the economy is less than GDP. Although this view is increasingly popular on the left—including among many UBI advocates—it still remains a minority view among economists.

7. de Soyres, Santacreu, and Young, "Demand-Supply Imbalance."

Chapter 57

1. See, for discussion, Peter J. Boettke and Adam Martin, "Taking the 'G' out of BIG: A Comparative Political Economy Perspective on Basic Income," *Basic Income Studies* 6, no. 2 (January 19, 2012), https://doi.org/10.1515/1932-0183.1218.

2. Larry Dewitt, "Research Note #19: Social Security Benefits as a Percentage of Total Federal Budget Expenditures," *Research Notes & Special Studies by the Historian's Office* (June 2003), https://www.ssa.gov/history/percent.html.

3. Congressional Budget Office, *The 2021 Long-Term Budget Outlook*, March 2021; and Office of Management and Budget, *Historical Tables, Budget of the United States Government, Fiscal Year 2022* (May 2021).

4. Mancur Olson, *The Logic of Collective Action: Public Goods and the Theory of Groups* (Cambridge: Harvard University Press, 1971).

5. See James E. Meade, *Agathotopia: The Economics of Partnership* (Aberdeen: Aberdeen University Press, 1989), 45; George D. H. Cole, *Money: Its Present and Future* (London: Cassel, 1944), 147.

6. James M. Buchanan, "Can Democracy Promote the General Welfare?," *Social Philosophy and Policy* 14, no. 2 (1997): 165–79.

Chapter 58

1. Karl Widerquist, "Polls Indicate Support for Basic Income Increased from 8-to-1 Against to 3-to-1 in Favor between 2011 to 2021 | BIEN — Basic Income Earth Network," *Basic Income Earth Network* (blog) (November 4, 2021), https://basicincome.org/news/2021/11/polls-indicate-support-for-basic-income-increased-from-8-to-1-against-to-3-to-1-in-favor-between-2011-to-2021/. Another poll from 2020, however, showed that a majority of Americans oppose a UBI, 54% to 45%. See Hannah Gilberstadt, "More Americans Oppose than Favor the Government Providing a Universal Basic Income for All Adult Citizens," Pew Research Center (blog) (August 19, 2020), https://www.pewresearch.org/fact-tank/2020/08/19/more-americans-oppose-than-favor-the-government-providing-a-universal-basic-income-for-all-adult-citizens/.

Chapter 59

1. Erik Olin Wright, "Basic Income as a Socialist Project," *Basic Income Studies* 1, no. 1 (January 28, 2006), https://doi.org/10.2202/1932-0183.1008.

2. See Daniel Zamora, "The Case Against a Basic Income," trans. Jeff Bate Boerop, *Jacobin* (December 28, 2017), https://jacobin.com/2017/12/universal-basic-income-inequality-work.

Chapter 60

1. One of the most vocal conservative critics of the UBI was Henry Hazlitt, who was especially critical of Richard Nixon's attempt to implement a kind of Negative Income Tax in the 1960s (see chapter 61 for discussion). See, for instance, Henry Hazlitt, "Income Without Work," *Foundation for Economic Education* (July 1, 1966), https://fee.org/articles/income-without-work/; Henry Hazlitt, *Man vs. the Welfare State* (New York, NY: Arlington House, 1969).

Chapter 61

1. Ingrid Robeyns, "Will a Basic Income Do Justice to Women?," *Analyse & Kritik* 23, no. 1 (2001): 88–105.
2. Barbara R. Bergmann, "A Swedish-Style Welfare State or Basic Income: Which Should Have Priority?," *Politics and Society* 32, no. 1 (2004): 107–18.

Chapter 62

1. See, for instance, the breakdown by ideology in Hannah Gilberstadt, "More Americans Oppose than Favor the Government Providing a Universal Basic Income for All Adult Citizens," Pew Research Center (blog) (August 19, 2020), https://www.pewresearch.org/fact-tank/2020/08/19/more-americans-oppose-than-favor-the-government-providing-a-universal-basic-income-for-all-adult-citizens/.
2. High levels of redistribution seem to be entailed by the two principles of justice set out by John Rawls, probably the most important liberal political philosopher of the 20th century. See John Rawls, *A Theory of Justice (Original Edition)*, 1971, 19.
3. This point is developed in great detail by Karl Widerquist in his *Independence, Propertylessness, and Basic Income: A Theory of Freedom as the Power to Say No* (New York: Palgrave, 2013).
4. Robert Greenstein, "Commentary: Universal Basic Income May Sound Attractive but, if It Occurred, Would Likelier Increase Poverty than Reduce It," *Center on Budget and Policy Priorities* (June 13, 2019), https://www.cbpp.org/research/poverty-and-opportunity/commentary-universal-basic-income-may-sound-attractive-but-if-it.

Chapter 63

1. For an overview of the nature and history of libertarian thought, see Matt Zwolinski and John Tomasi, *The Individualists: Radicals, Reactionaries, and the Struggle for the Soul of Libertarianism* (Princeton, NJ: Princeton University Press, 2023).
2. See Murray N. Rothbard, *For a New Liberty* (New York: Collier, 1973).
3. Many libertarians and neoliberals associated with the Mont Pelerin Society engaged in vigorous debate over the merits of a UBI. See, for a helpful overview, Daniel Coleman, "Getting Tough or Rolling Back the State? Why Neoliberals Disagreed on a Guaranteed Minimum Income," *Modern Intellectual History* (June 8, 2022), 1–28, https://doi.org/10.1017/S1479244322000257.
4. Milton Friedman, *Capitalism and Freedom* (University of Chicago Press, 1962).
5. Friedrich A. Hayek, *Law, Legislation and Liberty, Vol. 3: The Political Order of a Free People* (London: Routledge & Kegan Paul, 1979).

6. Matt Zwolinski, "The Libertarian Case for a Basic Income," *Libertarianism. Org* (blog) (December 5, 2013), https://www.libertarianism.org/columns/libertarian-case-basic-income.

7. Matt Zwolinski, "Property Rights, Coercion, and the Welfare State: The Libertarian Case for a Basic Income for All," *Independent Review* 19, no. 4 (2015): 515–29; Miranda Perry Fleischer and Daniel Hemel, "Atlas Nods: The Libertarian Case for a Basic Income," *Wisconsin Law Review* (2017), 1189.

8. For an overview, see Hillel Steiner, "Left-Libertarianism," in *The Routledge Companion to Libertarianism*, ed. Matt Zwolinski and Benjamin Ferguson (New York: Routledge, 2022).

9. Henry George, *Progress and Poverty* (New York: D. Appleton and Company, 1886).

10. See Daniel D. Moseley, "A Lockean Argument for Basic Income," *Basic Income Studies* 6, no. 2 (January 19, 2012), https://doi.org/10.1515/1932-0183.1216; Peter Vallentyne, "Libertarianism and the Justice of a Basic Income," *Basic Income Studies* 6, no. 2 (January 19, 2012), https://doi.org/10.1515/1932-0183.1224.

11. For a discussion, see Matt Zwolinski, "The Welfare State," in *The Routledge Companion to Libertarianism*, ed. Matt Zwolinski and Ben Ferguson (New York: Routledge, 2022), 311–24; Miranda Perry Fleischer, "Taxation," in *The Routledge Companion to Libertarianism*, ed. Matt Zwolinski and Ben Ferguson (New York: Routledge, 2022).

Chapter 64

1. Milton Friedman, *Capitalism and Freedom* (University of Chicago Press, 1962).

2. Jyotsna Sreenivasan, ed., "A Statement by Economists on Income Guarantees and Supplements," in *Poverty and the Government in America* (Santa Barbara, CA: ABC-CLIO, 2009), 269.

3. See, for discussion, Amity Shlaes, *Great Society: A New History* (New York: HarperCollins, 2019), chapter 10.

4. See Milton Friedman, "Welfare: Back to the Drawing Board," *Newsweek* (May 18, 1970), 89, https://miltonfriedman.hoover.org/internal/media/dispatcher/214056/full.

Chapter 66

1. Philippe Van Parijs and Yannick Vanderborght, *Basic Income: A Radical Proposal for a Free Society and a Sane Economy* (Boston: Harvard University Press, 2017).

2. Evelyn L. Forget, *Basic Income for Canadians: From the COVID-19 Emergency to Financial Security for All* (Toronto: James Lorimer & Company, 2020).

3. Karl Widerquist, *Independence, Propertylessness, and Basic Income: A Theory of Freedom as the Power to Say No* (New York: Palgrave Macmillan, 2013); Karl Widerquist, *A Critical Analysis of Basic Income Experiments for Researchers, Policymakers, and Citizens* (New York: Springer, 2018).

4. Robert Wright and Aleksandra Przegalińska, *Debating Universal Basic Income: Pros, Cons, and Alternatives* (New York: Springer, 2022).

5. Chris Hughes, *Fair Shot: Rethinking Inequality and How We Earn* (London: Bloomsbury Publishing Plc, 2019); Rutger Bregman, *Utopia for Realists: How We Can Build the Ideal World* (New York: Little, Brown, 2018);

Annie Lowrey, *Give People Money: How a Universal Basic Income Would End Poverty, Revolutionize Work, and Remake the World* (New York: Crown, 2018); Guy Standing, *Basic Income: A Guide for the Open-Minded* (New Haven, CT: Yale University Press, 2017); Guy Standing, *Basic Income: And How We Can Make It Happen* (New York: Pelican, 2017). Andrew Yang, *The War on Normal People: The Truth About America's Disappearing Jobs and Why Universal Basic Income Is Our Future* (New York: Hachette Books, 2018); Andy Stern, *Raising the Floor: How a Universal Basic Income Can Renew Our Economy and Rebuild the American Dream* (New York: Public Affairs, 2016).

GLOSSARY

Alaska Permanent Fund Dividend, or PFD—A cash payment issued to every Alaskan resident since 1982, regardless of their age, wealth, employment, or family status, and funded by wealth generated by Alaskan oil. Payments are based on the average financial return of the oil fund over the previous five years. Typically, distributions are around $1,600 per person per year, but they have ranged from a low of $331 in 1984 to a high of $2,072 in 2015.

Child Tax Credit, or CTC—A tax credit in the United States designed to assist low-income families with children. As currently structured, it provides larger benefits to families with earned income, while still providing some benefits to parents who are not employed in the formal labor market. In addition to phasing in with work, it also phases out for middle-income taxpayers and disappears completely for upper-income taxpayers.

Children's Health Insurance Program, or CHIP—A program that provides comprehensive health insurance coverage to low-income children that is funded jointly at the state and federal levels but administered by the states. Some states administer CHIP through expanded Medicaid benefits; others through a separate CHIP program; and some through a combination of the two.

Earned Income Tax Credit, or EITC—A tax credit in the United States meant to reward work. Depending on family size, it provides a tax credit equal to a percentage of a worker's income, up to a ceiling amount. The size of the credit remains level until earnings hit another threshold, at which point the credit gradually phases out with each additional dollar of income until it reaches zero. Many European countries have similar credits, often referred to as "in-work" credits.

Effective marginal tax rate—The tax rate that, in practice, applies to one's next dollar of income or wealth due to the combination of explicit taxes like income taxes and the phasing out of welfare-type benefits with each additional dollar of earned income. For example, a wage earner who faces an income tax rate of 25% and who will also lose 10 cents of benefits for each dollar earned faces an effective marginal tax rate of 35%, since losing 10 cents of benefits per dollar earned is equivalent to an implicit tax of 10%.

Electronic Benefit Transfer, or EBT—the mechanism by which many welfare benefits, including TANF and SNAP (defined below), are transferred to beneficiaries in the United States. Beneficiaries receive physical cards that work like commercial debit cards to which benefit funds are automatically deposited. Recipients swipe their cards at checkout, like any other debit or credit card, and the system deducts their purchases from their balance.

Family Assistance Plan, or FAP—A program proposed by US president Richard Nixon in 1969 and inspired by interest in the NIT (defined below). Even though it had a work requirement of sorts and only covered families with children, the FAP is the closest we've come to a national UBI.

Internal Revenue Service, or IRS—The US taxing authority, which administers numerous transfer programs that are styled as tax credits in addition to collecting revenue.

Manitoba Basic Annual Income Experiment, or MINCOME—A pilot program that took place in the city of Dauphin, Canada, from 1974 to 1979. A family that earned no other income received a payment equal to 60% of Canada's threshold for "low-income;" every dollar earned from other sources reduced this benefit by 50 cents. The results of the MINCOME experiment were uncovered forty years later by economist Evelyn Forget.

Means test—To "means-test" or to "use a means test" is to limit the benefits of transfer programs to individuals or households under a certain income or wealth threshold. Sometimes this is done by gradually phasing out benefits once a threshold is met, other times a means test precludes participation altogether once the threshold is met.

Medicaid—The major program for providing free or very low-cost health insurance to low-income individuals in the United States. It is funded by both federal and state taxes but administered at the state level within federal guidelines.

Medicare—A health insurance program in the United States for seniors and some younger disabled individuals regardless of income. Beneficiaries must generally pay for part of their care through deductibles and other payments, as is also usually the case with private insurance. It is funded by federal taxes on wages and is administered by a federal agency.

Negative Income Tax, or NIT—A UBI-like program popularized in the 1960s and 1970s. Anyone with income *over* an exemption amount pays tax on that income, while anyone with income *under* the exemption amount receives a transfer from the government equal to some percentage of the unused exemption amount.

Organization for Economic Co-operation and Development, or OECD—An intergovernmental organization composed of thirty-eight member countries, primarily but not exclusively from North America and Europe (along with Australia and New Zealand). Member countries are generally high-income, developed countries with market economies and democratic governments. The OECD aims to identify common problems and best practices (such as tax policies) for addressing those problems, as well as to provide coordination among member country policies.

Section 8—The main federal program in the United States for providing housing assistance to low-income individuals. Recipients find their own rental units on the private market, and then the government pays a portion of their rent directly to the landlord. The subsidies are often referred to as "Section 8 vouchers."

Social Security Administration, or SSA—a US federal agency which administers the retirement and disability benefits described below.

Social Security Disability Insurance, or SSDI—A program offered by the SSA that provides benefits to disabled workers and family members that meet certain requirements. Beneficiaries must have worked a minimum length of time in the recent past and paid FICA or SECA taxes on their earnings (defined below).

Social Security Old Age and Survivor's Insurance, or SSOASI (sometimes simply "OASI")—A federally funded pension-type benefit for retired workers in the United States. This is the main program offered by the SSA, and what people mean when they simply refer to "Social Security." Current workers pay taxes that are specifically earmarked for Social Security formally titled FICA (Federal Insurance Contributions Act) or SECA (Self-Employment Contributions Act) taxes but often referred to as "Social Security" taxes or "payroll" taxes. Eligible retirees receive benefits determined by the amount of past earnings and the age at which they begin drawing benefits. Although most people believe that their past taxes fund their specific future benefits (much like a regular pension), this is not true. Taxes imposed on current workers fund the benefits of current retirees. Widows, widowers, and dependent children of deceased workers are also eligible for benefits.

Special Supplemental Nutrition Program for Women, Infants and Children, or WIC—An additional US anti-hunger program for pregnant, postpartum, and breastfeeding women; infants; and certain children up to the age of 5. WIC provides physical vouchers that beneficiaries redeem for a small list of pre-approved foods at participating grocery stores. Like SNAP, WIC is federally funded but administered by each state.

Supplemental Nutrition Assistance Program, or SNAP—Colloquially referred to as "food stamps," SNAP is the second-largest anti-poverty program in the United States. Low-income individuals and families receive benefits monthly on a debit card that they may use to purchase approved foods at participating stores. Like many US benefit programs, SNAP is conditional upon working or looking for work. However, it is not limited to families with children nor only to extremely low-income individuals.

Supplemental Security Income, or SSI—A third program offered by the Social Security Administration, which supplements the standard SSOASI benefits for "people with limited income and resources who are disabled, blind, or age 65 or older." These benefits are not based on prior work experience and are financed by general Treasury funds rather than the payroll taxes collected specifically for Social Security.

Temporary Assistance to Needy Families, or TANF—The US program that is closest to what people typically think of as "welfare." TANF provides block grants to states, which in turn operate programs designed to help low-income families with children. These programs have work requirements and time limits, and generally deliver aid through EBT cards (defined above). Federal law and often state law impose restrictions on where beneficiaries may spend these funds.

Universal Basic Income, or UBI—A program of unrestricted, unconditional, and (at least ostensibly) universal cash transfers. Also known as a Basic Income, a Citizens Dividend, a Basic Income Guarantee, a Guaranteed Income, a Citizens Income, a Social Income, or a Social Dividend. A **UBI-plus** is a UBI layered atop existing programs; a **UBI-minus** is a UBI that replaces some or all existing welfare programs.

INDEX

For the benefit of digital users, indexed terms that span two pages (e.g., 52–53) may, on occasion, appear on only one of those pages.